DISPLACEMENT DAY

When My Job Was Looking for a Job

A Reference Guide to Finding Work

Thomas B. Dowd III

Award-winning author of *The Transformation of a Doubting Thomas: Growing from a Cynic to a Professional in the Corporate World* and *From Fear to Success: A Practical Public-speaking Guide*

Copyright 2014 © Thomas B. Dowd III

Note: The views expressed are my own and not those of my current or former employers.

—Thomas B. Dowd III

All Rights Reserved

No part of this book may be reproduced or transmitted in any form by any means: graphic, electronic, or mechanical, including photocopying, recording, taping or by any information storage or retrieval system without permission, in writing, from the authors, except for the inclusion of brief quotations in a review, article, book, or academic paper. The authors and publisher of this book and the associated materials have used their best efforts in preparing this material. The authors and publisher make no representations or warranties with respect to accuracy, applicability, fitness or completeness of the contents of this material. They disclaim any warranties expressed or implied, merchantability, or fitness for any particular purpose. The authors and publisher shall in no event be held liable for any loss or other damages, including but not limited to special, incidental, consequential, or other damages. If you have any questions or concerns, the advice of a competent professional should be sought.

Manufactured in the United States of America.

ISBN: 978-1503053656

Praise for *Displacement Day*

"This book shows you how to get the job you really want in any market, at higher pay than you might have thought possible."

— **Brian Tracy** - Author, *No Excuses*

"Tom masterfully takes the readers on an emotional and motivational roller coaster that will relate to anyone going through the pain of losing a job. What sticks out most is the quick transition from empathy to action. The specific direction from the author leads to a path of success."

— **Justin Sachs, Best-Selling Author of** *The Power of Persistence* **and** *Ultimate Business Mastery*

"Tom's latest book is full of golden nuggets of wisdom, insight and common sense advice. Open any page and you'll find something to help you live more purposefully and lead more bravely."

— **Margie Warrell, Forbes Columnist, Bestselling Author of** *Find Your Courage* **and** *Stop Playing Safe*

"I like to say that 'a setback is a set up for a comeback.' Tom Dowd is living proof of this! In *Displacement Day*, Tom shares his formula to come back from job loss. This isn't a theoretical book, it is the author taking you on his professional journey through job loss using the formula he very successfully applied. Lots of people talk the talk, what I respect most about Tom is that he WALKS THE WALK, *Displacement Day* is further proof of this!"

— **John Brubaker, *Award-Winning Author of* Seeds of Success *and* The Coach Approach**

"Thomas Dowd has captured the sense of fear and doubt that comes with losing your job. More importantly he has defined a way to take one of the biggest situations of your life and turned it into the biggest opportunity of your life. This book is a must read for anyone who has been downsized, right-sized or removed from their position. Following this process you will find hope, purpose and success."

- Ron Finklestein, International Author, Sales Coach and Creator of the *businessgrowthexperience.com*

"As a subject-matter expert in the use of LinkedIn and other tools needed to succeed in the business world, I was highly impressed with how the author simplified the approach for people looking to build a plan to find a job. We are fortunate today to have conveniences, such as social media, to assist us, but many people still ask, "How do I start?" Mr. Dowd shares the power of this potential outreach while giving readers the confidence that they will land in the right place and find success."

- Donna Serdula, author of *LinkedIn Makeover: Professional Secrets to a POWERFUL LinkedIn Profile*

"I'm going to buy several copies to share with job search clients. Tom's storyline puts perspective on the job search journey while providing realistic and tangible job search tips that will prove helpful to anyone. Tips that I found especially important: network, network, and network some more; turn your passion into your career; let go of your past; and, "Apply if Greater Than 50 Percent" (I really like that one!). Thank you, Tom, for sharing this valuable advice and personal journey in this useable format!"

- Mary Kozicki LaFontaine, Manager, Lewiston (Maine) Career Center

"Tom Dowd has first-hand experience of his subject and writes with both clarity and expertise. In today's world where wannabes are plentiful and the blind pretend they're qualified to lead the blind, Tom's competent focus on doing what works is exactly what you need to find a new occupation."

- Cris Baker, Author of *Self-Sabotage? What it is, Why we do it, When we do it, How to Overcome It!* and *What you Resist, Persists!*

"*Displacement Day* is a must-have book for everyone because history has proven that we never know when our day of unemployment is coming. Tom applies his extensive coaching skills to create a comprehensive guide to one of the greatest professional challenges we can face, losing a job. He details every step in the process of moving forward in your career and in life!"

- **Neal Williamson, HR Professional**

"*Displacement Day* is transformational. Just when you thought the pink slip was a ticket to the unemployment line, you realize instead that it's a golden opportunity ticket. This is the beginning of a new journey and your career guide. Thomas Dowd is here to help you focus on your new role of finding and connecting to your next position. With practical, real world tips and insights, Dowd shares his success strategies during a challenging time all while keeping your head held high. If you are like many professionals who have been through corporate reorganizations, sudden changes, or part of the business landscape that is shedding old paradigms and blooming with new innovative growth, make the commitment to be bold, step out of your comfort zone and move forward with confidence knowing there is a bright future ahead of you."

- **Stephanie Checchi, Channel Marketing Program Manager, CA Technologies**

"*Displacement Day* is not your average self-help business resource, just as generosity is not a word that jumps to mind when thinking about out-of-work job seekers. But Tom Dowd has been on both sides of the hiring desk, and generosity informs his work and this book. Realizing that even out of work you have much to offer others in the same boat, as well as to everyone in your network, may come as an invigorating revelation to many a disheartened job hunter."

– **Hannah Tays, Food Industry Professional**

"Having stepped out of the examples that Tom has outlined so well, I can now relate to some of the mistakes I could have avoided had I used *Displacement Day* as a reference. I will recommend this book to others in the professional world as a terrific reference tool. Many of the tips Tom outlines we know but in the "heat of the moment" forget. This would serve as a good reminder of those important baby steps we all should be preparing for - well in advance of 'D-Day'."

- **Karma O'Donal, HR Professional, Camden, Maine**

"*Displacement Day* is a great example of the power of networking and the critical positive mental attitude it takes to deal with a corporate downsizing and find a new job/career in today's environment. Social media like LinkedIn may have changed the tools used today but nothing is a substitute for preparation, due diligence, and determination when making a career change."

- **David Ciullo, President of Career Management Associates and the Host of the national HR Power Hour radio show**

This book is dedicated to anyone who has ever had the unfortunate, or fortunate, task of finding a job. I say *fortunate* because you may actually learn something about your character and resolve during the process that will change the course of your life and career.

Foreword

Displacement Day: When My Job was Looking for a Job immediately resonated with me, having found myself in a similar position in 2008. What? Twenty years of dedication, delivering, leadership, and results led me one morning to an invitation to a conference call where the entire sales and marketing departments were terminated effective immediately—"and here is two weeks' severance." Shock is an understatement, especially when I was hit with a rather sizeable mortgage that couldn't be handled by one spouse's income, investments that were underwater, and exhaustion from giving 110 percent of myself to this company. Now, I had to go into adrenaline-fueled action mode to survive. Where does one find the strength, perspective, positivity, focus, determination, and confidence?

I wish I'd had Tom's book in 2008 when my *Displacement Day* hit. Tom effectively captures both the rollercoaster of losing a job and finding a new one, while providing very tangible and actionable suggestions to help find the best job for *you*!

What's obvious in any job search is that you excel at some things and not others. For example, if you are a great networker, but need to work on your follow-up, there's a chapter just for you. If you are extremely organized and working hard to send out ten résumés a day, but find it difficult to connect with the people you're sending them to, then there are great insights for giving you the confidence to get out there and network. Maybe you're someone who is just stuck on *what's wrong with me?* and are having a lot of doubts about what value you bring and what your unique brand may be. Regardless of your situation, Tom provides action steps to get you moving in the right direction and help you identify your strengths.

This book is unique because unlike others out there on job search or transition, Tom makes the job search manageable by breaking it into bite-sized chapters, enabling you to jump in and out depending on your unique job-search issues. The book is a hands-on reference guide that sets the tone that ensures you will be able to get through this experience with a little guidance. You can come back to it every day and find solutions quickly to ensure the most effective job-seeking days!

One message that comes through loud and clear consistently in Tom's journey is the need to know what you want, including identifying your goals and writing them down, focusing on them, and having an action plan to get there. If you don't have clear goals, it's like driving your car without a steering wheel—how far will you get?

If you long to get where you need to be in the shortest period of time to land the job that you really want, start reading now!

Best of luck!

Michelle Chung
Co-Author, *On Track: More Success, Less Stress in 10 Minutes a Day*
and co-owner of mPWR10 Partners, LLC.
www.mpwr10.com

Contents

1. My Beautiful Funeral 5
2. Introduction 8
3. Acknowledgements 10

Dust Yourself Off and Get Started

4. Take Time to Absorb It 16
5. Don't Let Your Past Hold You Back 18
6. Make Luck Happen 20
7. Build Your Castle 21
8. Don't Decompress 22
9. Answer the Critical Questions 23
10. Have Your Three Salaries Ready 24
11. Prepare for This Moment... Now 25
12. Have Your Résumé Ready... Now 26

Cast a Wide Net

13. Examine the Reliability of Your Network 28
14. Test the Predictability of Your Network 29
15. Make No Assumptions 30
16. Keep Old Connections Alive 31
17. Maintain Personal Support Circles 33
18. Be Thankful for the Support 34
19. Understand the Importance of the "Rolodex" 36
20. Go All-in on LinkedIn 38
21. Cast a Broad Net with a Narrow Focus 40
22. Take All Invites to a Free Lunch 42
23. Don't Miss Opportunities from Within Your Social Circles 43
24. Recognize the Gaps in Your Network 44
25. Ask the Last Question in a Networking Session ... 47

26 Know Your Strongest Connections 48
27 Get Recommendations Before You Need Them 49
28 Cross-Pollinate Your Network 51
29 Make it Obvious that Your Primary Networking Goal is
   Not to Find a Job 52

Dig Deep into the Process
30 Recognize There are No Guarantees 55
31 Build and Maintain Daily Routines 56
32 Attack the Bucket List, or at Least the Honey-Do List 58
33 Make Rejection Productive 59
34 Know that Your Résumé Isn't Perfect 61
35 Talk with People Who Have Been Through It 62
36 Know That Your Résumé Is Yours 63
37 Be Careful of Predators 64
38 Pull Each String All the Way Through 66
39 Marry Your Unique Talents 67
40 Be Clear in What You Want, Including the Level 68
41 Recognize the More Important Roles in the Job Search Process 70
42 Be Proactive with Follow-up 71
43 Be Realistic with Promises 72
44 Show How You're a Specialist 73
45 Get to the True Meaning Behind Headhunters 74
46 Know That Tenure is a Curse and a Blessing 76
47 Apply if Greater Than 50 Percent 78

Use All the Tools in Your Toolbox
48 Put Together Your Marketing Plan 80
49 Integrate SWOT Analysis into the Process 83
50 Institute Multi-Generation Plans into the Process 86
51 Track Everything 88
52 Avoid Supportive Words 89

53 Have Your Résumé Tell Your Story 90
54 Do Your Homework 92
55 Know Your Audience 94
56 Know Your Communication and Leadership Capabilities 96
57 Evaluate Your Finite Time 98
58 Call in Favors 99

Keep Moving

59 Get Over It 101
60 Stay Healthy 102
61 Be Open and Honest About the Situation 103
62 Enjoy the Rollercoaster 104
63 Continue to Help Others 105
64 Maintain Your Mentors 106
65 Be a Mentor 107
66 Find Outside Activities 108
67 Know What You Want 109
68 Be True to You 110
69 Turn Your Passions into Your Career 111
70 Break Out of Your Comfort Zone 112
71 Take a Different Route 113
72 Live for the Future 115
73 Don't Accept No News as Good News 116
74 Vent Out Loud 117
75 Lean on Your Support Group 118
76 Know Where Your Eggs Are 119
77 Fight Feelings of Isolation 120

Maximize Your Soft and Hard Skills

78 Be Detailed and Succinct 122
79 Listen Intently 123
80 Don't Be Shy with Your Résumé 124

81	Think About Consulting and Contracting	125
82	Find a Good Editor of Your Work	126
83	Be Bold	127
84	Practice Interviewing	128
85	Prepare Your Elevator Speech	130
86	Know that Every Interview is a Great Interview	132
87	Recognize Varying Priorities	133
88	Go Beyond Skills, Experience, Talent, and Tenure	134
89	Keep the Lines of Communication Open	135
90	Build and Maintain Your Personal Brand	137
91	Use Facts	139
92	Keep in Touch	140

Pertinent Chapters from *The Transformation of a Doubting Thomas: Growing from a Cynic to a Professional in the Corporate World*

93	Wait Three Months	142
94	Be Impatiently Patient	144
95	Build a Network	148
96	Be Yourself—the Paradox	153
97	Treat Each Day Like an Interview—Another Paradox	156

Effective Tools from *Powerful Professional Transformation: Unleashing Leadership Program*

| 98 | Determine What Interviewers Want… Dealing with Behavior-based Questions | 160 |
| 99 | References | 166 |

Transform into Who You Really Want to Be Professionally 167
Also by Thomas B. Dowd III 169
About the Author 171

Displacement Day

1

My Beautiful Funeral

Have you ever imagined your own funeral? Who will do your eulogy? Who will be your pallbearers? Will anyone show up or even care? I attended my own funeral. Let me explain. But before I do, I need to disclose that no one died or was injured in the making of this narrative.

On a typical day when I was happily playing solitaire and checking Facebook at work, I got the call. June 6th—the anniversary of D-Day. Not World War II; I'm talking about Displacement Day—the day my twenty-three-year job was eliminated. Just like that, it was over. Hard work, tenure, and skills weren't part of the cost-cutting decision.

On my ride to work on that fateful day, a news report announced that 175,000 jobs had been added in the United States, making the unemployment rate 7.6 percent. On my ride home I was on the other side—one of 11.6 million unemployed. To grasp the magnitude, take the entire population of New York City, and then add another 4 million people. The call was like a gunshot to the head. My work identity was gone immediately. I was being put to rest and people were preparing for my funeral. Condolences rolled in, hugs were bestowed, tears flowed.

What will people say when you're gone? An old manager once asked me if I ran through a wall, would people follow? At the time, I didn't know the answer. I *needed to know* the answer. That was a lifeline—a time for action. Fast-forward six years later to D-Day. I don't recall a more calming day. It was a day of self-reflection…a chance to hover over my dead body and ask if my life and career were a success. The notes flooded in. "Tom, you've touched me more than you'll ever know, personally and professionally." "Tom, we love you… This IS your next speech." I ran through a wall, and people followed.

How was I going to tell my three daughters that Dad was sent to the farm, just like my childhood dog? A spending freeze on shoes, clothes, and pizza may be worse than death for teenagers. My middle child's head tilted down at a mourner's angle and a small tear rolled down her cheek as if it was about to drop onto my coffin. My youngest daughter held me in a bear hug as if it was the last time ever, while my social-media-conscious sixteen-year-old daughter told me that all responses to relocation questions on Facebook were to be "no"—as if I had a choice. The denial, the anger, then acceptance—the exhaustive feeling of having my family watch my demise. However, my support system refused to let my casket be nailed down as they put in a crowbar made of emails, phone calls, and leads. I was being resuscitated.

How many of you have prepared a will? A will reduces stress and chaos. The *run through the wall* question six years earlier was my wake up call, but I didn't realize then how it would prevent my professional passing. My eyes were opened wide as I started to build an extraordinary career-saving and life-changing network. In Keith Ferrazzi's book *Never Eat Alone* he notes, "Build it before you need it." Real relationships built over the years provided me meaning, and are the reason for my success now. I wasn't six feet under. I was six degrees from Kevin Bacon, or at least six degrees from my big break. I was alive. My support system was my CPR.

My job loss became a celebration of life, not my funeral. It reminded me how deep my love and my appreciation really are for my family, friends, and network. I was not defined by my job. I defined my own life and was going to do my funeral my way. No, I'm not going to belt out Sinatra. I lost work but found me. I used my displacement as reaffirmation that when I leave this earth, I'm leaving with no regrets. Think about your own funeral—when your spirit is hovering over the mourners, will you leave them something to mourn and celebrate?

So, let's go back to the question: Have you ever imagined your own funeral? Who will do your eulogy, who will be your pallbearers, who will care? My eulogy was shouted out by the many key people in my network who blew my trumpet for me and gave humbling accounts of the person I had been, and who I had become. My pallbearers carried me when I couldn't go any further. The overwhelming flood of calls and messages showed who cared. I have to admit that I started writing this narrative immediately after I got the call, and I wrote the end too. We all know we're going to die—I don't mean that "end." I mean the speech ending, where I get a job. I wrote it before I had a job secured. It wasn't overconfidence, it was just a belief that I was surrounded by an ironclad network that refused to stop giving me the oxygen I needed to survive. Are you ready to see your own funeral? I lived to see mine, *and it was beautiful.*

2

Introduction

After twenty-three years with the same company, I got *The Call That Nobody Wants*. I had already started Thomas Dowd Professional Development and Coaching, LLC, as a side job in 2011, in which I taught groups and individuals how to effectively transform into who they really wanted to be professionally using tools like interviewing, networking, and résumé writing. I was in somewhat of an ironic situation, my credibility as an expert in professional development suddenly at stake.

The irony started within a few hours after my job was eliminated, with a pre-scheduled speaking engagement for an organization called "Jobs for Maine Grads." It continued into the next week, when I landed a radio interview on a show where I had tried to discuss my previous two business books several months before. When I told the producer of this satirical twist, he invited me to immediately come onto the program to discuss unemployment in Maine.

How was I going to keep my emotions in check enough to keep a clear head? I've been an active member of Toastmasters International since 2008, and have always found that writing speeches and journals keeps me sane. I used the same approach when the potentially disastrous call came, starting with a jobless journal and notes to reflect my feelings, documenting what I had learned, and helping to keep a clear path to the ultimate goal: a job. "My Beautiful Funeral" passage that started the book is a version of a speech that I wrote within minutes of getting that call. This speech and subsequent book are the lessons I learned on this very personal journey. My passage through unemployment lasted fifty-nine days. I tell you this because my path to land it took many turns. It felt like an eternity until the relief set in with the job offer. I'm convinced that the relatively short period of time was due to having a clear plan and a support system that I now want to share. A journey I would never wish on anyone, but am so thankful that I took.

This book takes you on the rollercoaster ride, from buying the ticket to the moment your stomach sinks thanks to those quick drops, to that final race to the end, arms raised in jubilation. What I've found with rollercoasters is that many riders get on for the thrill of not only surviving, but the adventure of something that pulls you between fear and excitement. Your own ride is in front of you. Though you may not have chosen this particular ride, your reaction while you're on it is up to you. You may ask yourself, "How can I even imagine the possibilities of a new job when I'm panicked about paying my mortgage and providing for my family?" We can get there together—you're not on this journey alone. What if instead your question became, "Can I land an even better job?" The answer is, "*Yes.*"

3 Acknowledgements

This book is a reference guide for anyone dealing with unemployment, whether you may be out of work yourself or you know someone going through this massive life change. One of the comments that hit home for me was from a former colleague who said, "It's a lot easier dispensing advice on how to find a job when you already have one." That may be true in many cases, but I was writing this book as I was going through the unemployment process. I wanted the immediate teachings to hit the paper in order to ensure that all the mistakes I made or heard about during the process were documented. I liked the realism of the statement above and learned to appreciate what people sacrificed to move me ever closer to the job I was seeking. I preferred practical advice rather than the countless times I heard a version of, "Every time a door closes, a window opens." I say this not with mock contempt or a lack of appreciation for the sentiments, but I would get an awkward feeling that people were feeling sorry for me. I wanted movement in my pursuit of a new job—not sympathy. I wanted and needed to take action to achieve this goal; I had no time or energy to waste. Paradoxically, the *window* comments ultimately did come true. For those who said it or thought it, thank you from the bottom of my heart for teaching me another lesson. I wasn't simply getting *sympathy*. I was getting the *support* I required to move me forward on this journey.

I want to acknowledge my family, friends, and colleagues who never lost faith or confidence; the people who believed me when I told them I wasn't worried. I meant that. I wasn't worried, not even a little. As mentioned in the introduction, it wasn't overconfidence. It was a belief in my ironclad network. Besides, if I couldn't believe in myself, why should anyone else? I want to thank Kim Mitchell, who said immediately after I heard the news, "I'm only worried about you for the next two hours." Meaning, the tone and attitude for the next couple of hours would influence decisions, next steps, and my approach for the long haul. She was right to ensure that my head was on straight and that I was laser-focused on my goals. I made the choice to not even leave the parking lot before the road to my new job began. I placed a phone call to a fellow Toastmaster member of a local club that I was coaching. I heard they had a training manager opening. Thus, the search began. After I finished the call in the parking lot, I moved a couple of thousand feet up the road and walked into the office of a company managed by a former boss where my skill set could potentially be used. As I saw it, I could wallow in sorrow and angst, or I could make the effort to resolve this *little bump in the road*.

When I got home on the evening of June 6th, I sat down with my children and said, "My job going forward is to find a job. I promise to put as much passion, energy, and commitment into this job as I have for the last twenty-plus years." I held myself accountable to make sure my kids had as much confidence in me as I did. Thank you to my children for never questioning those words.

I want to thank everyone who responded back to an email, phone call, or conversation, even when they felt they weren't helping. Some people said that they had no openings and would keep my information on record—and actually did, as I continued to get leads months after the fact. Thank you for following through and giving me hope and opportunities.

My sincere appreciation goes out to the people who gave me valuable advice that provided me with the confidence to go through this potentially stressful situation, even if that advice came years before. I will hold on to their wisdom forever. In no particular order since every piece of it was valuable, thank you to: Steve Crawford, Jeff Schmidt, Erin Dymowski, Steve Dymowski, Christine Duffy, Nichole Kelley-Sirois, Greg Sirois, David O'Connell, Everett Berger, Frank McKelvey,

Sherry Reid, Neal Williamson, Dick Jacobs, Chip Rossi, Steven Cohen, Dave Ciullo, Mary LaFontaine, John Brubaker, Wende Stambaugh, Joy Bollinger, Leslie Johnson, Gregg Davis, Joe Claricurzio, Carmen (Felix) Garte, Joe Grondin, Sandra Hachey, Beth Hennessy, Joni Lindstrom, Jim Kokocki, Wendy Harding, Cynthia Martin, Wayne Mercer, Deb Nowak, Nita Pital, Kishore Sashthiri, Augie Schau, Hilary Schau, Kristine Smith, Cynthia Wheeler, Donna Tutty, Jo-Anne Walton, Jasen Wood, Lori Wood, Adria Minevich, Jeanne Gallagher, Lynne Snow, Trevor Koenig, Ted Dwyer, Tami Chester, Jeneen Marziani, Karen Salisbury, Anne Casey, Amy Vitale, Navroze Eduljee, Julia Caslin, Alfred Manganiello, John Echternach, Shelley Waite, Todd Beacham, Michael Quinn, Joan Pappas, Patrick Strieck, Noreen Dow, Parker Chamberlin, Beth Chamberlin, Amy Perkins, Michelle Chung, Brett Lerner, Robyn Reisinger, Kevin Burns, Mike D'Andrade, Joe Hickey, Frank Cerullo, Maria Harris, Robin Chacon, Kathy Bernath, Shane Flynn, Jim McGowan, Heather Bentley, Jeff Nathan, Kristi Christman, Rich Wagenknecht, Don Danese, Vin Contento, Marie Drouet, Gwen Ellis, Jim Kane, Monal Pathak, Robert Hayes, Christine Channels, Eric Inkrott, Chrisine Comune, Karl Andersen, Mary Jo Anderson, Lori Macchi, Katy Emmi, Scott Macchi, Jarett (J) Isralow, Bill Bowlsbey, Chris Cusack, Mike Kinane, Tom Cyr, Elizabeth Hamilton, David Hamilton, David Berez, Kim Devlin, Blanca De La Rosa, Jeff Dobbs, Mark Pearce, Luke Donaldson, Dave Edelson, Jenn Ehresman, Danny Bader, Chris Hogan, Nadine Stillmunks, Mike Battagliese, Krista Wrona, John Caruccio, Jamie Danner, Jim Biniasz, Ed Hawthorne, Dina Kanabar, Marshall Bonaquisti, Devin Farmer, Jill Engel, Ryan Conner, Michael Curtis, Branan Cooper, Christine Costagliola, Steve Stark, Mignona Cote, Shawn Harris, Scott Bailer, Mark O'Donal, Karma O'Donal, Doug DeSimone, Ryan Cobb, Shawn Leger, Kelly Cahill, Terrence Cahill, Steve Ryder, Kris Rosado, Steve Bescript, Paul Mosley, Barry Baird, Bob Shiflet, Jessica Andrews, Bob Lamantia, Josh Reitzes, Patrick Rockenbach, Michelle Zander-Brown, Darryl Fincher, Rob Cochran, Brad Dunckel, Rich Coombs, Warren Butler, Tim Gayhardt,

Brian Burbage, Tewksbury Library, Lewiston (Maine) Career Center, J.V. Fletcher Library, and to the countless others I may have inadvertently left out.

To the people who provided recommendations when they were needed and even when they weren't, your words meant a lot. I am humbled by the praise and appreciate the time and effort it took. Special thanks to Christian Pieri, Tammy Wagenknecht, Greg Purinton-Brown, Louise Nail, Pam Moyer, Bob Ferland, Joyce McPhetres, Dax Cummings, Jeff Sargent, Heather Perkins, Carl Duivenvoorden, Elizabeth Cagnon, Wes Strader, Tim Wescott, Corey Fogarty, Mark Foster, John Reddy, and Sandy Cox.

From the very first "official" networking session with Ben Ryan, to Ron Becker, Dan Chappell, Todd Cunningham, Ingrid Petrus, Ana Ness, Janice McCreary, Annie Witthoefft, Pam Marsh, Jack Mahoney, John DeSantis, Brian Gray, Sandy Wood, Russ Zusi, Mary Lynn MacKenzie, Angel Birch, Karen Humphries, Ellen Schwartz, and many others, I am appreciative of the invested time.

I want to send my thanks to my first set of eyes on the first version of *Displacement Day*—Polly Hall, Hannah Tays, and Kathleen FitzGerald—who turned the very rough first draft into a presentable manuscript. To my editor Jen Blood, I've said it before and I'll say it again: Thanks for bringing my words to life.

I'm indebted to social media such as Facebook and LinkedIn for making the job search so much more bearable. I'm not sure how this process was before these tools came along, but I'm thankful that I don't have to find out. I want to thank my old Toastmasters club in Belfast, Maine—Dirigo—for their continuing support when I was no longer with the company, and for my new Maine clubs in Bangor—Bangor Toastmasters—and in Waterville and Augusta—Kennebec Valley Toastmasters—for being so welcoming.

Finally, I want to thank the clients of Thomas Dowd Professional Development & Coaching, LLC who could have easily questioned how someone can teach people job-search techniques such as interviewing, résumé writing, networking, and professional growth when he didn't have a job himself. You didn't run away. Instead, you ran to me because you knew I could empathize, and you gave me the credibility I was hoping for. Thanks for recognizing the win-win situation.

Dust Yourself Off and Get Started

4   Take Time to Absorb It

The amount of time it took to read the title of this chapter is about the amount of time it took me to flounder around wondering, "What now?" If you have been laid off or find yourself suddenly out of work for any reason, I suggest taking enough time to take a deep breath and ensure you don't make any unnecessary emotional decisions or actions that may burn bridges. I actually invested the time between packing boxes and saying goodbye to formulate a thoughtful email as my departing gift to my now-former colleagues. Prior to sending, I made a point to ensure that it was positive, balanced, and could not be misinterpreted as over-the-top emotional irrationality. Below is the majority of the message:

"Change is inevitable, growth is optional." – John C. Maxwell

I found out this morning that my job was eliminated—it's effective immediately. After twenty-three years with this company, I can only say, 'thank you.' I am who I am professionally based on the bumps, bruises, and triumphs this company has provided me. I can't thank all of you enough for transforming me into someone who can leave this company with his head up. I'm also hoping that it is temporary. I feel great about my prospects and know that I will land in the right place.

I've attached my résumé for you to review and feel free to send it to anyone you feel would like to see it. Please also forward to anyone whom I may have inadvertently missed in my rush. I've also attached a letter I wrote a few days after my first books were published in September 2012, to our company's CEO as I was bursting with pride about where I'd been individually and where I saw this company moving in the future. My feelings for this company have not changed—it is full of success stories.

> *"There are no defining moments. There are only moments for you to define."*
> *– Tom Dowd*

I then attached a letter that I had sent to our CEO earlier in the year. This letter was a note that discussed the negative media attention the company had been receiving at the time. It emphasized the fact that the individuals within any company are what make it special. My message to him was that the company, regardless of the media scrutiny, had a multitude of employees working hard to get past it. Below is the last paragraph:

"I bring up the timing, because you know more than anyone the angle the press likes to take with "too big to fail" and the "one percent." What the sometimes negative media fails to recognize is the efforts of the 260,000 employees working behind the scenes to offer the right financial solutions to our customers. Yes, we make mistakes. The question is, can we learn from these mistakes to be better people, better employees, better community partners, and a stronger organization because of them? I think we can. I think there are more people in this company who are forging ahead every day to make a difference for themselves and for others. I wanted you to have these books as a symbol of growth, a symbol of support, and a symbol of success that we are strong. The company has winners. I am but one of the many success stories at (this company)."

I couldn't have been too far off with my sentiments. I received a note from a former colleague asking if I contributed to the new marketing campaign for my now former company that started six months later. The theme surrounded the message of learning from our mistakes and building personal relationships. I can't say that I contributed directly, but I've learned over time that relationship building is critical for success for everyone.

Don't Let Your Past Hold You Back

I was the type of person who bled the colors of my employer. After eighteen years, the financial institution I'd been working with was taken over by another company; there went that color. Similarly, I've had friends and family over the years who, in varying degrees, have defined themselves by their jobs. When meeting someone for the first time, they are often the type whose first question is, "What do you do?" The answer to that question generally revolves around employment. I've found with some people that the question is more than idle chitchat: their world revolves around their work identity. I'm not talking solely status, role, or compensation—I'm talking about the whole package of work identity. That means that when he or she loses a job, his or her whole world dissolves—or at least that's the way he or she feels.

The question you must ask yourself in similar situations is: are you asking to be polite, are you starting a conversation, or are you truly defined only by the job that you do? Personally, I want to be proud of the company I work for, but I don't believe a job should define me—it should be a piece of me. I was fortunate enough among side business interests, volunteer work, and the overall broadening of my horizons in recent years, to truly no longer feel that what I did for work defined who I was. That mentality was profoundly helpful when I lost my job. As a result, the line in the opening speech, "I wasn't defined by my job. I defined my own life….I lost my job but found me," was easy to write.

I was trying to imagine if I would have had the same mentality even five years ago. I'm not sure. What I am sure of now is that my job is only one chapter in my life. I've never had an issue with putting my heart and soul into a job, so I don't feel like my loyalties for my employer will be at stake. My job is an important chapter for sure, but it's not my only chapter.

Make Luck Happen

Sitting around waiting for the phone to ring only happens when you've taken the first action to send a note or make the initial call. You can *hope* for something to happen, or you can take action and make it happen. I do believe in luck, but only after I've gotten the ball rolling. We have to be vigilant enough to push our own success along by taking the initiative to make our own luck.

7 Build Your Castle

Everett Berger, an executive coach and leadership development professional, provided the following sage advice:

1. Let go of the past.
2. Build your castle first. Tap into a vision for yourself.

This comment is a reference to how Walt Disney built his castle first, before he built the entire kingdom.

3. Tune out all the noise and voices.

This comment references the need to concentrate and focus. Your job is to look for a job. Focus on the right priorities.

Don't Decompress

Frank McKelvey, an old manager of mine from way back when, took time out of his personal vacation to invest time with me. He provided the following astute wisdom:

1. The time that you spend decompressing is time when jobs are passing you by. "People who got busy on 'Day One' increased their chances of landing a job sooner. It sounds obvious, but it's not always practiced."
2. Spend time with the family to assess what is wanted. It's not a *me* thing, it's a *we* thing.
3. Package your thoughts on your résumé.

"Don't light the whole stage…light your particular character." As much as we want to be everything to everybody, we can't, so we need to narrow our path to highlight our best characteristics.

Answer the Critical Questions

Success is contingent on clearly knowing what you want and coming up with an action plan that will get you there. It's important to anticipate the questions you must answer for yourself, your family, and your potential employer:

1. Location: Are you willing to relocate? If not, what's the longest distance you will travel?
2. Satisfaction: Will you enjoy the type of work you are pursuing?
3. Compensation: Do you know the lowest acceptable compensation offer?

You may not get exactly what you want for all three. You may even need to do the pros and cons exercise to come up with suitable responses that you can confidently believe in and convey. The general rule of thumb I had for myself was to be satisfied if I could fulfill two of the three criteria specific to location, job satisfaction, and compensation. However, again, you must be prepared with your own answers and be able to confidently articulate them. You may say to yourself, "I will accept two of the three," or "I will only accept all three," or, "I will take what I can get as long as I get one of the three." Then, you must answer which of the three you will accept. This comes with some internal soul searching, some budget planning, and some deep conversations with any other parties impacted by your decisions. Until you understand what you truly want and need, you can't realistically be prepared for a job search.

10   Have Your Three Salaries Ready

Didn't I just mention in the last chapter that you should know your lowest acceptable compensation offer? So, you may be asking where the other two salaries come from? Sometimes we can't get what we want, while other times we undervalue our services due to what we perceive as desperate circumstances. If you land with the right organization, you should be paid in close proximity to your worth. However, only you define that worth, and you need to be ready to negotiate. In some cases, you must be willing to walk away. The three salaries you must know are:

1. Your dream job. What is your high end of the scale?
2. What is the acceptable range? What are you worth based on your experience, your skills, and the job for which you are applying? You must do your homework.
3. What is the absolute lowest, drop-dead number that can be put on the table that you will still accept? You obviously won't start negotiations with this number, but you need to be prepared for it.

As for negotiations, you must assume that every company negotiates. Be prepared for that, and don't simply take the first offer without some discussion. Some companies may not negotiate, but it's always worth asking rather than assuming. Even non-management positions most likely work within a range.

11 Prepare for This Moment... Now

Are you prepared for this moment? If you even hesitated to answer, it's time to start preparing yourself. As stable as we think we are in any employment situation, including your current position if you are employed, that situation can change at any time. You must plan for the worst-case scenario or valuable time will be wasted as you scramble to figure out your next step. If you are scrambling, don't forget about the emotional rollercoaster you'll be on—meaning your head won't be on straight and your thinking will most likely not be clear to start the process. Whether you are in a seemingly stable job now or you're out of work at this moment, do you know your strategy? What's your end game? What are your immediate and long-term goals?

It's important to have a clear vision—in writing. When we are in scrambling mode, we make quick decisions, rash judgments, or we go back and forth between strategies and actions we want to execute. To avoid that, investing time to clarify your goals ahead of time will be beneficial because it provides a map to follow. This is your playbook, giving you the tactics needed to get where you want to go. Once you write it all out, it starts to feed and expand the vision further, which will only help. Try not to become so focused on your targeted goals that you lose sight of the peripherals, such as maintaining a strong network. Written goals, however, have been proven time and time again to exponentially increase success. It's okay to also have multiple paths on this journey—AKA Plan A, Plan B, and Plan C—but the more clearly laid out the paths are, the more you can proactively take the actions needed to get you to your end goal.

12 Have Your Résumé Ready... Now

If you're fortunate to have a job currently, I still suggest having your résumé ready now. Within minutes of the fateful call, I was circulating my résumé around the company, which jumpstarted my search and, subsequently, my chances of success. Résumés are fluent and ever-evolving documents; I recommend setting up a recurring quarterly appointment to keep yours fully updated. You should never have to scramble or invest time to do this with any urgency, as urgency increases the risk of mistakes and can show disorganized thoughts. Being ready now reduces or eliminates these risks, while showing potential employers how prepared and diligent you really are.

Cast a Wide Net

13

Examine the Reliability of Your Network

I'm sure you've heard legendary football coach Vince Lombardi's quote, "Hope is not a strategy." That definitely applies here. You can't *hope* that your list of "friends" and "connections" on your social networking sites will bail you out of your bind. If you've compiled your network by simply sending out invitations to LinkedIn, for example, you may be in for a rude awakening if there is a real need to tap into the network. You need to redefine networking. A solid foundation is built on mutual, lasting relationships—not merely checking off the box. I intentionally put quotes around friends and connections because you must ask yourself how truly connected you are with them. Having a large volume of connections will not get you a job if those connections don't really know you, your skill set, your potential, or in some cases, even who you are. If you're unsure of how people see you, it's time to find out. Start now to deepen the relationships you have with these connections in order to create a more reliable network. Let people get to know the real you—the whole you, not just the business you.

How do you start? It's simple: send a note, or make a call to a connection. The connection can be from LinkedIn, your contact lists, Facebook, or any other means through which you have a name, phone number, or email address. We'll discuss various strategies throughout the book, but the important thing is to get past your hesitation and start to turn your contact list into a reliable network. These conversations will build credibility, trust, and respect, and formulate a meaningful—and mutual—relationship that will last. You want the conversation to end with that connection truly knowing you're there for him or her.

14 Test the Predictability of Your Network

On the day I lost my job, I jumped on LinkedIn and asked for recommendations from over 200 connections (see sample below). The first one I received back within minutes was from an old boss with whom I hadn't always seen eye to eye. We never found the formula to work well together, but what did I have to lose by asking? The recommendation was well thought out and was a positive account of our time together. He also added a note inviting us to get together if I needed anything else to help in the process. The exercise of looking for recommendations with nothing to lose was a great early lesson in testing the unpredictability of assumptions I made about my own network—something I talk more about in the next section, "Make No Assumptions." "Testing the Predictability of Your Network" will also give you a way to gauge what people will say if contacted as a reference.

Sample LinkedIn recommendation request:

Dear (Name),

I'm sending this to individuals I've recently (choose a relevant topic: worked with, coached, mentored, etc.). In light of the recent announcement of my job being eliminated from (Company A) due to budget cuts, I'm asking for recommendations to add to my LinkedIn profile in order to continue building my brand and credibility. If you have any questions, please let me know.

Thanks in advance for helping me out. -Thomas B. Dowd III

15   Make No Assumptions

Interestingly enough, some people I would have bet my new job's salary on as most likely to respond to my request, never sent a note back or returned my call. I learned not to be surprised, for a variety of reasons: people may have been scared for their own jobs; people may not have known what to say, so they used silence; I might have had the wrong contact information (e.g., I found typos in some of my contact information); people were on vacation or out of the office; or people didn't always keep up with updating their own contact information on social media sites (e.g., LinkedIn). In all cases, I hold myself fully accountable for not having established a more predictable relationship during the networking process. I needed to follow up more often, and maintain stronger ties to ensure contact information remained current. Networking is not a check-the-box exercise. Like any strong relationship, it takes ongoing work and maintenance. The work becomes harder if you are making up for lost time. I stopped being surprised when I didn't get return calls, and instead set in motion action plans to get more creative in my attempts to contact people—meaning I didn't rely solely on emails, I tried contacts at different times, and I followed up.

It's important to understand that you are not stalking or annoying people in your attempt to contact them. However, by holding myself accountable, I was digging down deep in questioning how accurately I understood my own network. We get too comfortable, at times, in our dependence on our network by thinking it truly is a net. It is a net only if we weave it properly, using people we can depend on. Stop making assumptions about your own network and start being an active part of it. You will build mutually stronger and deeper relationships.

Keep Old Connections Alive

Although I had revisited older contacts occasionally over the years, my own job search made it clear how essential it is to keep those older network contacts alive. In routine networking sessions, I've gone back to past colleagues, for example, to "reinvent" myself if they had a negative perception of past work. However, the number of contacts I had that I hadn't been in contact with, in some cases for over ten years, was a wake-up call. I realized that merely having names on a list was not a network. I needed to keep old connections alive, so I started to go back and rebuild those relationships. I didn't want a snapshot from over ten years ago—or even just a couple of years—to be the lasting image we had of each other. I found rekindling the professional relationship created some great memories and was an easy transition into getting to know each other again.

How do you go back to someone you haven't worked with or spoken to in years and say, "I need you"? First, reframe the question: is it really about need, or is it about *want*? I started by thinking I needed to speak to people to help me in my pursuit of a new job, but quickly realized how much I wanted to catch up with those people. Even if an old contact is in a different business field or a different company, the phone call can still be made. When I was talking with colleagues from the distant past, I found people had selective memories. The conversations tended to lean toward the good times or the progress we'd made since we last talked, versus some potentially rocky times we may have had. By restoring past professional relationships, I found I was improving personal relationships and enhancing dormant ones. The process of reinvigorating the network was a great exercise in reformulating opinions about my former colleagues and myself, and infusing old relationships with mutual trust and respect.

How do you go about sending that out-of-the-blue email or making the potentially *awkward* call? This is no time to be hesitant. It is only as awkward as you make it. Avoid phrases like, "Sorry to bother you," or, "I know we haven't spoken in over ten years…" It's important to clearly state your objectives, and one of them is to reconnect with past colleagues—or business partners, clients, etc. Don't be afraid to be vulnerable enough to share what's happening to you professionally and what you hope to glean from the networking session. You shouldn't be looking for sympathy, but you should be straightforward. A recurring theme throughout this book is the understanding of the importance of knowing the wants and needs of others you've crossed paths with in the past. If you don't know, it's alright to ask the question directly, "What can I do for you?" In the most selfish of situations of needing a job, thinking of others can be a mutually strong tool for long-term success for both of you. You shouldn't intentionally be looking for reciprocity. Instead, every conversation should be a mutually flowing conversation of genuine interest in which these former colleagues and contacts have been since you last connected. It's alright to be a little nervous until you get comfortable. You will find that these conversations happen each day in business and after a couple of sessions, you'll gain confidence.

17 Maintain Personal Support Circles

Of course, we all have our usual social circle. Many times, I found myself too tired or unmotivated to catch up with them while I was unemployed. It's easy to come up with excuses after a significant life change like being laid off. You may not be feeling sociable, or maybe you don't want to spend unnecessary money. I agree with the importance of paying attention to the budget, but when you're invited to a friend's house, I suggest going if you can—even when you don't want to. You need a social support circle as much as a professional network at this time. This is less about having people feel sorry for you, and more about having a needed break or distraction. You may even find a few fresh ideas coming from those who know you best.

18 Be Thankful for the Support

I've had numerous sympathetic conversations with people saying, "I wish there was something I could do for you." I tried my best to be gracious and thankful for the thoughts and support. Then, I let those people know that they could help simply by forwarding my résumé and marketing plan to anyone and everyone they felt might benefit from it. I surprised myself with how broad I allowed others to reach for me. Broad-reaching is not the same as desperation. I was anxious to get a job, but more importantly, I was open to taking chances with other industries where I may have had less experience. It opened me up to companies that had creative and innovative cultures receptive to individuals who could make a difference, regardless of that individual's background.

By taking specific action, your support system does more than just be there for you. I had numerous unexpected business prospects come to light because someone knew someone who knew someone else. I've always been thankful for this type of assistance, but I often waited passively for it to happen. I had to start asking directly for assistance to have someone pass my information on to others. I was putting those who cared the most about me to work—and it was worth it. In reality, I knew it wasn't really too much effort to send a quick email or make a simple phone call to connect us together. I had learned that I was passively making assumptions when I really wanted action taken. As previously stated, hope isn't going to make my needed connections. I learned to make it clear what I wanted. When done professionally, I didn't feel I was pushy—I was just moving along someone's "wish" that there was something they could do for me. Conversely, I knew how much better they felt about themselves for being an active part of the team effort. Helping to facilitate the future direction for someone should make them feel good. As noted in the acknowledgements, I am so appreciative of my entire support system.

19 Understand the Importance of the "Rolodex"

The traditional "Rolodex" may not be the same as it used to be, having been replaced in large part with new tools like Facebook, LinkedIn, Outlook, Google, and other social media platforms and repositories of contact information. That doesn't mean maintaining—or even starting to build—that contact information is any less important now than it ever was. If you currently have a job, start or continue to build your network now, using all of the aforementioned tools at your disposal. If you're currently unemployed, it's time to play catch up. Watching multiple unemployed people just starting to build their network in desperate times may exacerbate your own anxiety on the road to employment. It's important to realize that the process is not insurmountable. The tools available to facilitate the information-gathering process are critical to your success, and make it easier than ever to begin the process of networking. It's time to build your "Rolodex."

I had several traditionalists say they wanted face-to-face meetings and phone calls. Those are fantastic if you can get them, but don't depend on them. Networks are built in many different ways today. There is no set formula, but social media and email often are the most convenient ways for the recipients of your requests to connect. It's important to get to know what the people you are depending on are using as their own "Rolodex," whether it's LinkedIn or something else. If you need to create new social media profiles, then do it. It's important to adapt to new technologies and networking practices if you're not already there. While I'm not typically a conformist, my own circumstances meant that I needed to go with the easiest means of connecting. If the people I was trying to connect with preferred one method over another, my goal was to make it as easy and convenient as possible for them. In this case, I recognized that if everyone else was doing it, there had to be a good reason why.

On a personal note, I know how time consuming social media can be. I think it can become habit forming and has the potential to keep you from developing real relationships. However, I can comfortably say that more than eighty-percent of my time using social media was on LinkedIn, or working with the contact list that I've maintained over the years in Microsoft Outlook. I considered this invested time crucial to setting up the meetings that would become real conversations. The time-consumption question is really about productivity. How productive are you when you're using it? It wasn't as important for me to view a post of what someone had for dinner last night as to better understand what was going on in his or her career and industry.

As you continue to reach out to people, build your Rolodex by capturing contact information through incoming email signatures and other means such as business cards, websites, and letterheads. Most professionals have some type of email signature that often includes their phone number and address. I significantly increased the number of times I was able to capitalize on new leads by taking down the information in those email signatures. I even found valuable opportunities with administrative assistants' contact information when it came to setting up networking sessions, interviews, and meetings.

20 Go All-in on LinkedIn

I soon realized that my chances of getting a job increased exponentially when I utilized LinkedIn as a tool. The use of LinkedIn may not be the best course of action for everyone. For example, if you are looking only at small businesses locally, it may be easier to go into each specific organization to set up an appointment. However, even with this example, it is prudent to at least glance at LinkedIn to see if the owner has a profile. LinkedIn has become so important as a networking tool that business-savvy individuals pay content experts to assist them in creating the most effective LinkedIn profile. A friend of mine, Donna Serdula, does this professionally, and has written *LinkedIn Makeover: Professional Secrets to a Powerful LinkedIn Profile*, a great reference book to help ensure that your own profile is the best it can be. If you're looking for specific strategies for making an impact on LinkedIn, I recommend checking out Donna's book.

By going "all-in," I mean doing more than replicating your résumé. Use more space to make a visual impact on your LinkedIn profile. You should make the assumption that recruiters and hiring managers will be looking for your profile after you have made contact—this assumption is a pretty good bet for many large employers today. If they don't find a profile for you, or find a quickly-put-together profile, that tells them a story. What story do you want told about you? Among the many candidates applying for jobs, a quality LinkedIn profile is a must to set yourself apart.

The basic free-service of LinkedIn is a great starting point and is often sufficient to meet most people's needs. LinkedIn does have Premium paid-membership with benefits that include a more advanced search feature, seeing who has viewed your profile, and allowances to send more messages. I will leave it up to your individual preferences and needs to determine if the investment is worth it to you.

21 Cast a Broad Net with a Narrow Focus

Keep all options open and cast a broad net. You may think you know what you want. In fact, I started this book *telling you* to make sure you know what you want. I wasn't lying, but I'm also realistic enough to know that that isn't always easy. It's acceptable to keep a somewhat narrow focus based on what you want or need, while at the same time keeping an open mind. In some cases, options may be restricted based on your established limitations, such as location. As you pursue these wide-open options, keep a narrow focus so that you're not drifting aimlessly, as that wastes time. For example, I had some conversations with companies in Boston, which is almost four hours away from my home. A commute would not be feasible for me, but I kept the conversation going until the companies said that there was no option to work remotely (work from home). Continuing down that path would have wasted precious time and energy. However, it was only after I confirmed the company's corporate policy that I gave up on that possibility. I include this example because I *heard* about another company that didn't allow people to work remotely. After doing some digging, I found that wasn't true. The ability to trust but verify, is an important tool in your arsenal. There is a difference between working desperately and working smart.

In casting your broad net, it's very important to market yourself to align with the specific job you are applying for based on the job description, the information provided on the application/job posting, and the details obtained from your due diligence. For example, as a speaker, trainer, author, coach, and banker, it became too difficult for prospective employers reading my information to decipher what role I really wanted when I applied to a new company. Although my answer was, "just about anything," that did come across as a bit desperate. I didn't feel desperate at all, but on paper it looked that way. I have always been able to find a way to enjoy my job and maintain a positive attitude, regardless of what I was doing. Over the years, I have learned the importance of being accountable to change what I don't like in my life or my work. But, how would anyone be able to get all that from my résumé? In some cases, even talking through it, I would laugh at how ridiculous it sounded without context. I might as well have just said, "I'm a people-person," and left it at that.

To avoid that kind of confusion, I had to align what I wanted with what I was going after. For example, I had recent experience overseeing banking risk. I know that the business of risk in banking is very important after the economic downturn in 2008 (or even earlier in some cases). My success in this type of role depends on my ability to be strong enough to come in with an objective point of view to push back, persuade business partners, and communicate effectively to identify and mitigate concerns. I made some changes to include more risk-based language on my marketing plan and résumé. I also built up the ways in which my side interests in speaking and training strengthened my ability to influence others when I had no direct power, while simultaneously refining my written and oral communication skills.

Although I had specific risk responsibilities with my former employer, I did cast the broader net to include operational risk, business controls, and even audit and compliance when applying for new jobs. My immediate goal was to get my foot in the door with prospective employers so that I could demonstrate how my diverse background would enable me to have an impact in the future of their company. I was able to do that enough to determine that the business of banking risk went beyond simply identifying issues, and was more about building strong relationships. Even though I had known that from past experience, I'm not sure how quickly I would have used it in networking sessions and interviews if I hadn't been dabbling in the other areas that weren't part of my direct expertise.

22   Take All Invites to a Free Lunch

Lunch may not always come with a networking session, but if you can make it happen, you should take advantage of it. There is value in meeting people face-to-face if the opportunity presents itself. It shows a more human side and builds deeper connections. I've found a large number of people sympathized with my situation and offered to take me to lunch. You don't have to ask me twice. In addition to getting out of the house and escaping the monotony that sometimes comes with job hunting, those lunches gave me an opportunity to meet new people and hear interesting stories and propositions. The power of an actual handshake in building trust and establishing deeper connections is also not lost. Interestingly enough, most of the in-person meetings had very little chance of leading to a job, but served to further emphasize the need to have a wide range of people and professions within my network.

 # Don't Miss Opportunities from Within Your Social Circles

When we talk networking, we instantly think in professional terms. However, I believe we should reframe that to include our inner circle and the people we hang out with the most. Adam Grant in his book *Give and Take* and Keith Ferrazzi in his book *Never Eat Alone* both reference the fact that our inner circles may be too close to us and too similar to us for us to depend on them *solely* to land us the *Big Job*. We often surround ourselves with people who have the same interests, have like-minds, have an emotional connection, and live geographically close. I found the same thing was true for me. However, that doesn't mean we should avoid social situations and stay in our cave until we find a job. If we feel comfortable enough with those in our social circle, that translates into more in-depth conversations that may give us valuable insight into our situation going forward. In addition, our inner circle may not give us the direct contact to get us the job, but I truly believe in the "Six Degrees of Kevin Bacon" theory, where a friend of a friend of a friend, and so on, will finally connect the dots for us. These types of conversations from within your social circle balance your approach and become a good starting point for your job search, while simultaneously providing a solid home base and support system, as needed.

24 Recognize the Gaps in Your Network

In the last chapter, I noted that we may be too close to our inner circle. We must reach beyond our inner circle and immediate colleagues so that all our eggs aren't in the same basket. We can maximize our network and strengthen our prospects by broadening and diversifying our reach. The most effective individuals also engage and target family and friends, along with professional groups, social circles, and even parents of children's friends, when possible. We want a sound and expansive platform from which to work, but there are inevitably whole populations of people we overlook in forming that platform. For me personally, I know I have blind spots and so must sit down and consciously think about who has been left out as I work to create the most far-reaching network possible.

Where are your blind spots? It's not an easy question, so ask the people in your circles specific questions about how to expand your network if you feel that it is too narrow, or you're missing people who should be included. Here are just some of the many potential questions to ask:

- Have I reviewed all of the business cards I've accumulated over the years?
- Have I gone through all of my current email contacts in detail?
- Are there people you know you've run into but can't remember his or her name, but remember someone who will know?
- Have you asked, "Who else should I connect with?" at the end of each conversation?
- Have you made your business colleagues and partners aware of your situation?

- Have you reached out to past mentors and mentees?
- Have you contacted current and past groups of interest? Personally, I instantly scoured my Toastmasters International and National Speakers Association contacts.
- If you have children in school, have you contacted the parents of their classmates? How many times has one of my kids come home and mentioned a job of one of their friends' parents. School directories and local phone books may be at your disposal.
- Review your social media contacts in-depth; review the recommended connections and start making requests to build your network.
- Do you have access to past meeting notes or to other communications (e.g., emails, memos) that may include the names of key contacts of people you've dealt with in the past or subject-mater-experts that may benefit you by setting up a meeting?

Even this tactic may not be as fruitful or productive as you expect if you are only asking the question of your immediate network—they too may be too close to you to see the big picture. We surround ourselves with people like us, which can be a blind spot in and of itself. There are more questions that you must ask:

- Are there ways to diversify your network? For example, have you found yourself talking to mostly men?
- Do you associate primarily with people in one industry?
- Have you stayed local in your networking efforts? Even if your desire is to remain local in landing a job, it shouldn't hold you back from talking with people outside your geographic area in order to gain a fresh perspective and expand your network.

It may be time to analyze what is missing from your own network. In addition to normal brainstorming techniques, I suggest putting your name in the middle of a piece of paper and from there jotting down streams of people you want to meet, asking the questions mentioned above. In addition, take a good look at your personal marketing plan to determine whether you have connections that align with your goals. If you don't, there is work to do to achieve your networking goals. Work is opportunity waiting to be unleashed. It's time to invest the time and effort to allow it to blossom and do some work for you.

 **Ask the Last Question in a Networking Session**

The question of all questions that must be asked in every networking session is, "Who else should I meet?" Think about the math. If you ask this question of three people and you get three names from each of them, you've expanded your network to nine. This easily turns into twenty-seven new connections, and the growth continues to expand. The opportunities are endless if that question is asked every time.

26 Know Your Strongest Connections

Friends and family are obviously strong connections—at least most of the time. Did you notice I didn't include colleagues? I have separated them because your strongest professional connections will change over time. Ask yourself who those connections were five or ten years ago. Chances are many names are not the same. When building your network, it's important to understand that fluctuations happen—players change over time. How important each one is to the other will also change over time. You need to either accept that reality, or make every effort to work on the relationship to ensure that it stays productive for both parties. Inevitably, some relationships may not stand the test of time, and that's all right.

In the meantime, you need to know who your most reliable connections will be, regardless of the business cycle. When the world's crashing in, who will pick up the phone for you? This section is very important to me because I made some assumptions about people who proved to be more fleeting network connections than the stable rocks I expected. To avoid that, I should have invested time building a deeper relationship with the people I *wanted* to be among my strongest connections. I had to imagine the receiver of my phone call or message when I absolutely needed something. I needed to be convinced that the call would get answered and the support would be there. If there was any question about the strength of that connection, I had some work to do.

Get Recommendations Before You Need Them

Even if you're deep into the job search, it's still not too late to put together your recommendations. You may have to make up some ground, but keep the effort moving forward. If you're poking around to see what's available on the job front and you're not on a full-blown job search, or you're simply looking for a promotion that needs character validation, now is the time to figure out who will recommend you. You don't want to be in the middle of filling out an application and get to the section about recommendations or referrals and be stopped cold because you don't know who you plan on selecting. I had several people in mind, but in some cases, it had been awhile since we last interacted. If you don't know the answer to the question, "Do I know who will endorse me?" then it's time to start writing out the list immediately.

After you finish the list of names, send a note or call the potential group of at least three to five people and ensure that they know they may be contacted. This may seem obvious, but I found that I didn't have complete contact information for a couple of people I wanted to use. I might have had an email address or phone number only. On some applications, name, address, email, and multiple phone numbers were requested. Be prepared. If you're building an online profile with a company that's general in nature, it may be okay to stop the process here.

As you start to narrow down the positions you are seeking and get to a point where a recommendation may actually be used, help the person providing the recommendation by giving them specifics about the job and the individual or types of skills the company may be looking for.

A targeted approach with the person doing your recommendation can potentially help the employer gather more meaningful information about you.

Finally, the personal and professional relationship you have with someone isn't the only criteria you should pay attention to when making a selection. Do you have connections that are brutally honest in all of their assessments? While that can be a great quality, you don't want all your strengths and weaknesses laid out on the table for your prospective employer. The person you select for a recommendation is an important part of the job search process; that person shouldn't spend the majority of the time talking about your less desirable qualities. A balanced approach is good, but you need to know ahead of time what's coming. Coach that person, if needed. I once went through a 360 feedback process where I included direct reports, managers, peers, and business partners in my feedback process. I was able to select them myself, so I picked the people I was closest to, thinking they would only sing my praises. In actuality, I had picked the people who knew me the best and were looking out for my best interests by providing critical feedback. Although this is not a direct correlation, understand that the people closest to you do care the most about you, but also know you the best. Additionally, it's important to be cautious about seeking recommendations from people who can only provide personal character responses. You want a balance of character information with business accomplishments.

28 Cross-Pollinate Your Network

Circles of friends and colleagues often differ. We have a circle of friends with whom we may like to talk sports, others may discuss politics, and others may be strictly about business. There may be some overlap, but we sometimes build protective cones around many of our circles. However, blending these circles can mean benefits for you and others. Your network is only as good as the work it is doing for all participants, so if there's an opportunity for crossover within some circles, take advantage of it. You may create the introduction for someone within your own circle to meet someone in your extended network. Or, you may ask if someone you are talking with knows someone in a particular field of interest that's outside the immediate circle.

The web of a network should have key members in it. When discussing networking, we often think of going straight to the top. Instead, it's important to make sure we are connecting with various levels within an organization. When we cross-pollinate our network, that network becomes more balanced, including friends, co-workers, former colleagues, doers, leaders, support staff, and even some fun personal network contacts.

 Make it Obvious that Your Primary Networking Goal is Not to Find a Job

Did I just read the chapter heading correctly? If you are out of work, you are considered jobless and most likely need to find a job. As the king-of-the-obvious, I just provided another *no kidding* comment. However, if you take a step back and reassess how you've approached any networking session while you are (or were) looking for a job, you might find that the first and last question you asked was related to, "Do you have any openings?" Even from someone like me who invests time coaching clients about the importance of having a goal outside of job searching, I found myself feeling the heavy weight of determining whether each networking session was a viable lead or simply a time to build a relationship.

We get led in this direction because we are the ones who take it this way. We might say it was tough losing our job, then sit back and wait for the sympathy to come in—even if unintended. I didn't want sympathy. As much as I wanted a job, I had to remind myself that my first thought was to build or enhance a connection, and not to cut to the chase of what was available in that person's organization. If someone on the street asked you, "Are you hiring?" you probably would look at them funny. Ultimately, if our primary goal clearly comes across as a job search, we are creating a wall. Instead, the goal should be to get someone to like you first. The rest will take care of itself through the developing relationship. Don't mistake me: I am not saying you should disguise your underlying goal of finding a job with a thin veil of insincere small talk. I'm clearly stating that your primary goal is not to find a job when you are specifically networking, but to make a connection.

If the goal is not to find the next opening while networking with someone, then what should you be doing? First, you must find the common bond—either personal or professional. Why did you think of this person in the first place? That most likely will provide you enough clues to find a link. You have to *relate* in some way to the person you're speaking with so it doesn't come across as a cold call. Whether it's a common field of expertise, or something you've picked up on LinkedIn, or the person who referred you to them, find the common ground. As much as we may inadvertently push the conversation into, "What can you do for me?" the success of the session is contingent on your ability to find *what's in it for the other person* to truly make a valuable connection—both sides need to get something from the conversation. Let the network find the job for you. You just need to keep the process moving by building strong relationships based on common bonds.

Dig Deep into the Process

Recognize There are No Guarantees

If I stopped everything I was doing expecting my best leads to come through, I would still be looking for a job. During my search, I interviewed for a job where I was given the impression, or misinterpreted the discussions in such a way as to believe, that I was a lock. Three weeks later, the company reorganized the department and the open job was cancelled. Luckily, I didn't have to learn this lesson the hard way. I continued my pursuit within minutes after that final interview. In another situation, I was told by a recruiter to call him before I accepted anything else because he had an opening that just needed to be finalized. I called a few times to follow up, but was told that, "Things changed." Things do change, and your best prospects are only as good as the lead you are pursuing at this very moment. Your job prospects turn to actual jobs when you start on the first day. When you recognize that all leads can be fruitful but that they are not guaranteed, you become more realistic in your views of the process and more motivated to keep moving until you have solidified your next position.

31 Build and Maintain Daily Routines

What's your plan for today? What about tomorrow? Have a game plan and a regular routine scheduled. *This is your job.* For example, you may want to set up the morning to review emails, spend the next section of the morning making phone calls, and the next section of the day sending out emails for potential networking sessions. You must have a daily goal, including writing a certain number of cover letters, dedicating time to review your résumé and marketing plan, looking at the openings at your highest prospect companies, and sending out a minimum number of networking requests.

Regardless of the action, building regular routines will keep you motivated when you wake up in the morning. If your first response when you wake up starts with you blankly staring at your computer asking, "What do I need to do?" then it's time to take a step back and establish a plan. You are most likely thinking tactically before you've thought strategically. Stop what you're doing and invest the time to set up a strategic plan*— even if it takes an entire day. The invested time of organization and time management will pay high dividends by making you more efficient and having a clearly formulated plan each day. In fact, this strategic day in establishing how the rest of your days will play out may be one of the more important days in the entire job-search process.

*A Strategic Plan will vary based on individual needs and preferences. Ultimately, it's your plan of attack. You may want to establish a priority of people you will be attempting to contact. For example:

- Go to family members (immediate and extended). Generate a list based on instant ideas.
- Call closest business friends. Generate a list comprised of immediate contacts.
- Contact friends not associated with the business you are interested in, but who may have ideas about the job-seeking process.
- Send emails/make calls to inner network: mentors, mentees, outside interest contacts (Toastmasters, local community/school, etc.), past colleagues—those with whom you have a strong familiarity.
- Contact people at companies you're interested in pursuing. Look at LinkedIn and other sources to obtain details.
- Continue searching LinkedIn, Facebook, and other social media sites with connections to look for secondary contacts.
- Go to known openings or known opportunities.
- Review job openings on LinkedIn and other sources (write down sources as they are obtained).
- Review LinkedIn contacts alphabetically.
- Go back to dormant contacts.

This list can go on based on your desires, and the order may be different for you. However, it should be your starting point. Then, decide how much time to dedicate daily to networking, sending emails to set up meetings, exercising, and other activities that will consume your day.

32

Attack the Bucket List, or at Least the Honey-Do List

I would typically put in a ten-to-twelve hour day of job-searching. I don't want to contradict the need to pursue the main goal—to find a job—but we do need to find balance. I am expanding on it as a distraction to break up your day. Take a lunch break and do a chore or address something you've always wanted or needed to do. A fellow unemployed friend wisely gave me the advice to at least take the weekends off to recharge. The amount of productive work goes down naturally, because not everyone is checking emails and messages, although I admit that many of the responses I did get were from people who slowed down enough from their own jobs to send a quick note or response on the weekends. You can partially control your own working schedule now that you're at home, so take advantage of it. Your spouse's honey-do list will appreciate it.

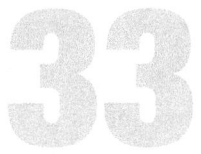

Make Rejection Productive

You will be rejected. You will have passive rejections, when people forget lunch meetings, or do not return your calls or emails. You won't get interviews you thought you should, and you won't even get a glance from jobs that you know you are qualified for. With the high unemployment rates, we have to get used to the fact that this unfortunately is normal. The reality is that there are far too many résumés flying around. Recruiters and hiring managers can't always filter or interpret them all accurately, quickly, or both. What you do with this rejection is another story.

When your phone is silent and your email inbox is empty, are you following up with past requests? When turned down, are you asking for feedback to become better the next time? Are you asking for suggestions for other possible leads? On several occasions, I was told that "other candidates were more qualified," that I was "over-qualified," or that I was "under-qualified," depending on the job and the people I was working through. In my conversations, I asked questions and was curious. The conversations that ensued led to times when I became considered for other similar roles, or for lines of businesses within that company that were not previously on the radar screen. I had circumstances when I was reconsidered after further discussion. My thinking is that one person creates an opinion of you based on the block of time that you spoke. Asking questions and possibly involving more people can get your name around, create new context to the conversation, and more importantly, keep you relevant. The goal is not to be over-the-top and in-your-face with the approach. The aim is to be curious, develop, and learn something for the next time around. If the next time around happens to create a path for you, you can look at it as a bonus opportunity. Even asking questions as simple as, "Who else should I talk to?" can turn rejection into your friend immediately. Rejection: expect it, learn from it, and then use it to move forward.

As a side note, you do need to understand that some people and companies may not discuss the "whys" of their decision-making process. Whether it is out of fear of being sued for discrimination, misinterpretation, or other reasons, it's important not to be discouraged if a request for feedback goes unanswered or is answered unsatisfactorily. The fact that you asked the question gave you the potential to gather some information to make you better, and is better than not asking at all.

# Know that Your Résumé Isn't Perfect

Having the same résumé for over nine years that I maintained each quarter provided stability and confidence to feel pretty good about it. It was used often in training classes and mentoring sessions, so I received plenty of solicited and unsolicited feedback. I used it as a template for what I taught others, and constantly made the adjustments based on the feedback I received.

I felt confident that my extensive experience in the financial industry was a positive attribute and started the first line of my profile with the statement, "Highly qualified executive offering over twenty-three years of…" However, a number of people let me know that the *executive* and *twenty-three years* comments may have priced me out of some roles and put constricting boundaries on opportunities. Even after nine years, I was getting new feedback! The opinions of some hiring managers may have been that I would be over-qualified for some positions, even though I would be satisfied with senior manager level positions of growth. It's not easy to change something you feel so comfortable with, but the revamped version received more attention and created more discussion. I'm convinced the new-and-improved résumé made a significant difference in how I was viewed on paper.

35 Talk with People Who Have Been Through It

You don't want to create an overflow of pity, but you can glean lessons learned from others who have been through it. Within three days of the infamous call, I was having lunch with someone who had been unemployed the year before and had landed a great job. Even as simple as him telling me to have lower expectations for contacting people in July due to vacation eased my mind about the process. With advice such as, I don't have to accept the first job offer, I was beginning to grasp the number of choices and the control that I had with the swirl around me. The level-setting discussion made me a little more "go with the flow" and patient during the summer months, while making sure that I knew my true value so I didn't get low-ball job offers. There is no need for you to reinvent the wheel. With millions of people who are or were out of work, you are bound to know someone who is going through it or has recently been through the process of finding a new job. In addition to the empathy, you will find insight from mistakes they may have made and can give you specific and actionable insight to run with.

Know That Your Résumé Is Yours

I've just written that you should be open to feedback on your résumé. I'm not contradicting myself when I also note that it's yours to make the final decision on how it looks and feels. Some of the feedback I received was negative. After taking in all that feedback, even though it was not always pleasant, I did listen to it. I then had to determine how much of it was related to style as opposed to influence and how much of an impact it would have on the decision makers who read it. People providing feedback is a gift—it is also an opinion. Many people base their thoughts on their own template. There is no perfect formula for résumés. Even when I teach résumé writing, I clearly have to articulate that my own résumé is a guide, and that their own résumés don't have to be an exact replica.

You should be conscious of the jobs you are applying for and ensure that your résumé meets the target and alignment of that job. However, there is no right or wrong résumé. To prove this, go to any search engine and put in the word "résumé" and see how many options pop up. The last time I did this in Google, more than 73 million results came back. You will find many varying opinions on résumés. In the end, *you* have the final determination of how you want your story told—and *you* must be comfortable with it.

37 Be Careful of Predators

Maybe the word *predator* is a little strong. I don't consider myself a full-blown sales and marketing person, so maybe I am a little more sensitive to this type of business. Immediately after I lost my job, some of the quickest responses I received from people with opportunities were from individuals involved in sales and marketing positions. Many were heavily commission-based with a bonus when they signed on new people. I remember years ago when a close friend of mine tried to get me involved in selling water purifiers. We agreed I would support him and go to one meeting; if I didn't like it, we would stop talking about it. I attended one meeting and instantly knew it wasn't for me. It was a business that worked well for him and taught him skills that would make him an eventual giant in the sales world. I knew it didn't match my skills or desires, but it was my first experience with multi-level marketing.

There are people with sales and marketing experience who would be perfect candidates for this type of position—people with an entrepreneurial spirit of independence who enjoy the adrenaline rush of knowing their success is purely contingent on the next sale. The number of instant responses I had from people in this type of field who were instantly on my calendar was amazing. Staying true to my mantra of casting a broad net, I listened objectively and asked enough questions to get a good feel for what was being offered. As I've mentioned before, it is important to stay open to all opportunities. I am being a little tongue-and-cheek with the chapter title, because I was doing something similar in trying to sell and market myself to others.

One of the key teachings was to be assertive enough to say "Thanks, but no thanks" if I was no longer interested. I found that persistency is a common trait in successful sales and marketing people. When I was pursuing jobs, I appreciated when someone said to me that they needed more time to think about it, or in some cases, that my follow-up in some cases was too much. Most professionals get it and will move along. I connected with many great people in what I found to be called the "level marketing" field, and respect the amount of time and effort it takes to really make it in that field. I also learned about persistency, assertiveness, and the drive to develop strong personal relationships in my own job search. Every connection can be a learning moment.

# Pull Each String All the Way Through

Leads are just leads until you bring them to life. Every networking session should end with, "Who else should I meet?" and, "Is there anything else I should be doing, or doing differently?" I was asked on many occasions during the job-seeking process if I knew a particular person. If the answer was "yes," I would set up an appointment with them. If the answer was "no," I asked if we could be introduced. Most times, I didn't try to keep it to a single business area or even try to determine how close the connection was—it didn't matter. What was important was that leads were being offered and it became my responsibility to do something with them. We have an opportunity to go beyond our immediate friends and past colleagues to tap friends of friends, long-lost relatives, and every other person who comes across our radar screen. If you have a lead, take advantage and send out requests to network. The ability to ask questions and find ways to connect the dots of your growing web of a network can be intriguing and fun. You might surprise yourself at how fruitful it is to be curious and pull that string all the way through.

Marry Your Unique Talents

I was fascinated by the networking conversation I had with John Brubaker, author of *The Coach Approach: Success Strategies From The Locker Room to the Board Room*. He and I had many common interests and hit it off right away, sharing notes about professional development. John turned on his coaching charm and we found instant connections as he shared his own stories of triumphs and tribulations when he was in a similar situation. He left me with the following information to chew on:

- Know your ideal job in the perfect world.
- Recognize your unique talents and passions. Pursue ways to ensure they are part of the job-search process to marry them with what you're looking for. You will be more motivated to follow a path of something that drives you.
- Figure out whom to get in front of to help you pursue these ideal jobs, unique talents, and passions.
- Know your strong general skills that can be carried with you and emphasized regardless of field.
- Sell the abilities and competencies that make up these skills in a targeted approach by aligning it to the jobs you're interested in so you don't come across as a jack-of-all-trades and master of none.
    - The jack-of-all-trades and master of none comment got my attention. I would ask people who knew me well and people I'd just met for their opinions of whether my story made me seem like more of a generalist or a specialist, and made appropriate adaptations based on their responses.

40 Be Clear in What You Want, Including the Level

Do you want to be on the frontlines with customers? Do you want to be a manager? Do you want to be VP of Marketing? Do you know what level is the lowest point you're willing to start in a new position and what future growth potential is available for the jobs you are seeking? With over twenty years in the financial industry, I knew clearly that I didn't want an entry-level position. There is nothing wrong with entry-level, but it needs to make sense with your background, tenure, and competencies. Also, not everyone wants to be a manager of people. Is the career path associated with the job you're looking into leading to a management role? You need to be clear in what you want—this includes the level.

The name of this chapter may seem redundant based on the rest of this book. To an extent, it is—but there are a number of aspects you need to be clear on when applying for a new job. If you rely on the assumption that you and your prospective employer are on the same page, you may well be disappointed. Within days of first losing my job, for example, I was offered a position with a local company, but it didn't match the role and level I was chasing.

In addition to the type of role you may want, you need to know what level you want. Being in the banking industry, SVP means different things to different people, including recruiters and hiring managers. Some companies hand out the title like it's candy while others limit it to only the highest levels. Looking from the outside in, it became obvious that my former company handed out SVP titles closer to the candy version. Don't get me wrong, I was proud of my promotion, but I was also proud of the many peers who also had the same level and title. One of the changes that I made on the résumé included removing that title.

As I mentioned, I was proud of my past accomplishment, but ultimately it didn't carry much weight on my résumé. Some prospective companies simply didn't have any of those types of roles open because they were few and far between since people in that position typically oversaw significant operations or employees, for example. I had that title when I managed many people; I had the same title when I was managing projects with no direct reports. I had to start speaking the *external* language of the companies I was pursuing, not the company I'd just left. That meant extra diligence in laying out what I wanted. The changes had to occur on my résumé, my marketing plans, my strategic plans, and in the conversations I was having. All forms of communication had to be moving in the direction of my laser-focused desires.

As a previous executive, I was still open to senior manager roles in order to get in the door, knowing I would put in the effort and attitude to get to the next level eventually. I needed to put that to paper so that everyone was on the same page. For example, on one of my marketing plans, I listed the following as my potential roles and options I was seeking:

Senior Risk Management Leader
VP, Operational Risk Manager, or
Executive SVP, Business Control, or
VP, Business Control Senior Manager

There was no question about what I was looking for and what opportunities could be presented. That description made it very clear what I wanted specific to the level of employment I was seeking and the type of role I was best suited for.

Recognize the More Important Roles in the Job Search Process

Obviously, everyone in our network has an important role to play. While it's important to avoid rash judgments about one contact being more important than another, I will tell you that if you have the choice between being in touch with a recruiter or a hiring manager, lean toward the hiring manager every time. The recruiters are there to screen applicants and determine who is best suited to move on to the next level of interviewing. While it's extremely important to have a strong relationship with them, if you have the contact information for the hiring manager, then use it. If you don't have his or her information, then do your due diligence and attempt to get it. I'm not condoning being pushy, but I am encouraging assertiveness. The hiring manager can provide exact expectations for the role, including the unwritten description. A hiring manager can provide insight as to what successful, and not so successful, people have done in the role in the past. Even if a hiring manager holds back some information, they now know who you are beyond your résumé. The contact also establishes a relationship that could be critical if there are equally qualified candidates applying for the same job. In that case, the hiring manager may even appreciate the extra effort you took to learn more about the job.

Be Proactive with Follow-up

People get busy. Let's be honest with ourselves—most networking sessions and conversations with people about possible jobs are more important to us than the person with whom we're talking. I heard many off-the-cuff comments such as, "Call me in a couple weeks." While I know most of us may give an instant response similar to, "Will do," I felt I was differentiating myself and ensuring action when I immediately put a follow-up appointment on my calendar. As with the last chapter, I wasn't going to be a pest, but I was diligent in making sure that I took full advantage of all leads. I couldn't afford to be skittish in my follow-up, and I found most people did not seem offended by someone who stayed on top of what we had discussed. Keith Ferrazzi notes in *Never Eat Alone*, "Don't apologize for being persistent." Persistency does pay off. Additionally, if you tell someone you will do something, such as sending your résumé or marketing plan, do it right away. You don't want to earn a negative reputation as someone unable to follow instructions or follow through on a task.

43 Be Realistic with Promises

Even the best-intentioned people make promises they can't keep. If I stopped looking for a job each time I was promised something, I would be years away from where I want to be. During a discussion at a local career center, I was once asked the question, "What do you do while you're waiting for the company to get back to you? They (the company) said it would be two or three months." I hope my response wasn't too sharp when I said, "I would call my next lead." Between having positions cancelled or being led to believe that I was the top candidate for a job only to find it had been given to someone else, I learned not to stop looking until I had an actual start date and a contract in hand.

One person in my network recommends having at least four serious leads. The definition of *serious* is not one that you hope will come to fruition, but one that you feel there is a real chance of landing. I agree for the most part, except I wouldn't put a number on it. I take an interpretation of a serious lead, well, very seriously, but I can't take it as an ironclad promise. My job looking for a job continued until I was 100 percent sure the job offer was made and accepted. Even on the day I received my most recent job offer, the HR person said they had to finalize a few things. I continued my search until the actual offer was in writing in front of me. I'm a trusting, but realistic, person—I know things change or that there can be miscommunication.

# Show How You're a Specialist

By averaging eighteen months per position for over twenty years, it clearly makes me a generalist. Being a generalist was great for my old company, but for many companies, getting hired happens when you're a specialist. I had several experiences in past roles where I had some expertise. During the job-search process was not a time to be shy about that expertise. There are few times in life where it is necessary to stand on the rooftop saying, "Look at me," and looking for a job is one of them.

There is a professional way to do this, however. You can give context and examples, but if you are not comfortable talking about your accomplishments, there are plenty of people out there who will have the advantage because they have no problem singing their own praises. I teach a session called, "It's Not Bragging if It's a Fact." Without being braggadocios, individuals can successfully talk about their accomplishments and bring them to life off the pages of the résumé. It's important to talk about how you can resolve conflict and work in a team setting, but it's also important to talk about your individual contributions in driving a business forward. You must talk about what made you a specialist and how that can set you apart from the competition. Have it come to the forefront with specifics. There's no "I" in team, but there is an "I" in interview, so make the most of it and learn to humbly—but confidently—speak about your accolades as a specialist.

Get to the True Meaning Behind Headhunters

During my job search, I set some goals with specific milestones and deadlines. I said that after a month, if I didn't see a definite lead on the horizon, I would start to tap into recruiters and headhunters to help with my job pursuit. I was fortunate enough to have a networking session with an old colleague who provided me with a list of recruiters he had used when he lost his job. I was excited to have this gift to get off to a quick start. Although I had heard about headhunters, I'd never truly understood what I was about to experience. My former colleague's gift led to my worst day in the entire job-seeking process.

I had mixed reactions when I sent out the original request to connect with the list of recruiters. Some never responded. I later found out that most recruiters are very specialized and target certain fields. This was good information to know. Others set up meetings that they blew off with no warning or communication. Others were downright rude via email and even in conversations, by making it very clear that they didn't want to work with me. I have to be careful with such a broad statement, because there were many that were helpful, polite, compassionate, and giving—but not all of them. However, even the polite ones cut straight to the chase. I found out quickly that I wasn't networking anymore.

After being frustrated for a call or two, I soon realized that recruiters and headhunters have a very specific job to do. If they were wasting time on a call with me because they felt I wasn't qualified for their particular niche or job, then they weren't making money. Once I genuinely understood how the relationships would be established, I began to appreciate both of our challenges and tried to step up my game by anticipating their very specific questions, challenging myself for the next similar call by doing more homework or better defining exactly what I was looking for.

I am very thankful for this frustrating piece of the process. When a recruiter calls they typically ask three questions: salary range, location preferences, and exact position in the exact field you're looking for. I began to take it as a compliment that I made their list to call. Knowing that they get a slice of the salary of the person they hire from the hiring company, and that they have a reputation to maintain in getting perfect hires for the companies that contract them, it became more understandable how some of the conversations went. As a job seeker, you're not required to deal with headhunters. Although I didn't run into it, I have heard from my career center friends, that there are situations when a recruiter is looking for the unemployed person to pay them to assist in the job search. I will caution you and say there are very few times *you* need to spend money on a recruiter or headhunter to get hired. However, if you choose to go with a legitimate recruiter, it is a choice you can make—just know the swarm of bees you're walking into… although bees are productive!

46 Know That Tenure is a Curse and a Blessing

Yes, employers want it both ways. They may advertise a position asking for only three-to-five years of experience, but have a description that looks impossible to do unless you have ten-to-fifteen years of this experience. Some of the reasoning is to keep the compensation expense reasonable. This makes good business sense, since there are more applicants than jobs and competition is intense. With over twenty years of experience in the financial industry, I started most of my conversations with that fact, thinking that the tenure would elevate my status. I quickly found out how careful I needed to be in communicating that information, because I was aging myself—and potentially increasing my price compared to the competition. I no longer wanted to lead with that fact.

Instead, I used a more targeted approach. As previously mentioned, I averaged eighteen months a position for twenty-three years, so I used language that made sense to the particular conversation. I batched some jobs together to elongate the experience level. For example, "I was in operations management for a total of five years." Instead of singling out each role separately where I had project management, risk management, and compensation management experience, this method does the math for the recruiter or hiring manager, instead of them having to add up all of my experience in different positions. By no means did I misrepresent myself, I just spoke the language and didn't invest so much energy into detailing how long I had certain responsibilities in each designated role. I became better at explaining the overall impact I had when I was in the role, which seemed to move me further into the conversation. The quality of the meaningful work that I executed and delivered became the higher priority—not the length of time spent doing that work.

47 Apply if Greater Than 50 Percent

As someone who has written up many job descriptions, what do you think I'm looking for? I'm looking for the *perfect* candidate, just like every other hiring manager and recruiter. The chances that I will find the perfect candidate are always slim. As I talked with fellow unemployed individuals, I discovered that many people read job descriptions and gave up without any further action. They made no call to the recruiter or hiring manager, and chose not to fill out applications for positions they were actually qualified for. Mary LaFontaine, who works for the Maine Career Center said, "Apply if you meet more than 50 percent of the job description." It is not an exact science or math equation. If you feel that you meet enough of the criteria, then go for it. Even if the "requirements" are not fully met, you should take a serious look at applying. I am realistic enough to know that perfect candidates most likely don't exist, but qualified candidates do. The ones who take the most shots increase their chances significantly. A colleague in the sales world used to say, "If one in ten buy, and you are only asking/offering to one in fifty…it's going to take you a long time to get that ten who say *yes.*"

Displacement Day

Use All the Tools in Your Toolbox

48 Put Together Your Marketing Plan

What do you want to do when you grow up? Does your target audience know your desires? Do you know your target audience? If you don't know the answers, it's time to figure them out. If you don't know what you want for yourself or how to market yourself, how can people help you get you what you want? Even for someone like me who teaches résumé writing, I had enough critical feedback from readers of my own résumé as being "too dense" or "too broad" to know that I had to make some significant changes. For example, that flexibility was easily identified as a marketable trait on my résumé since I averaged many positions in a short period of time at the same company. This *strength* of being flexible was a nice-to-have, but people making the hiring decision needed to know what competencies I had, what skills I possessed, and what I could do for them. The companies I was pursuing couldn't be expected to guess what path I wanted to take. I had to find a way for people to know that I was both flexible *and* competent. As much as I thought I was giving companies options, I found that they didn't have time to be too interpretative. The message is to still cast a broad net, but be more targeted with the approach so people know exactly what you want.

An effective way to be precise about what you want is by putting together a marketing plan. I used this tool in networking situations and found the murkiness cleared up not only for me, but for the people who could lead me where I wanted to be. You can still have multiple options based on your various pursuits, but the key is to have a targeted approach that aligns your skills with a field of work. The marketing plan can have fluidity for different fields you are looking into, but should be stable enough that you don't need one for every person you meet or for every different company you are looking into.

There are a variety of types and definitions of marketing plans. My advice is to look at the purpose of a marketing plan first, and keep it simple. The purpose is to make your goals as clear as possible to someone reading the document. The design of your marketing plan should be based on the harsh reality that someone may well glance at it for less than thirty seconds, so make the layout count. For example, you might put a clear statement expressing your interest at the top of the page, followed by examples of the types of positions you want to pursue, skills and/or competencies you possess, strengths, and accomplishments. It should be in a table format to pack a punch with an economy of words. In sessions that are truly networking only, you can also list all of the companies you are looking into so the person you're meeting with gets a sense of the direction you're taking. Your marketing plan can be adapted for different fields you are pursuing, but don't put yourself in a position where you're constantly revising it. My rule of thumb is that 85 percent of the story of you should remain the same regardless of the positions or fields you are looking into. Remember, the importance of a marketing plan is to market yourself in order to give someone a very clear picture of what you want.

Here is an example of a marketing plan:

Name:
Marketing Plan
Phone:
Email: LinkedIn Profile:
Website:

Marketing Statement / Profile

A highly flexible and experienced results-oriented, risk control-focused leader with significant financial industry knowledge, including: credit card, consumer lending, sales, service, ATM/Debit card, and risk management. Accomplished and talented manager with expertise in customer operations, risk assessment, compliance, business development, business analytics, business control, project management, business governance, and strategies.

Capabilities and Qualifications

Building relationships / collaboration	Influencing decision-makers	Risk control / assessment / mitigation
Analytics	Compliance	Communications (written, oral)
Project Management / Change Management	Executive presence	Business Support / administration

Personal Strengths

Decisive- utilize collaborative skills to make fact-based decisions. Uncompromising ethics.	Results driven- develop and implement innovative and realistic solutions.	Big picture thinking- logical and sensible in approaches to management, utilize common sense.
Inquisitive and curious- ask pertinent questions to get to the root of each problem that leads to sound decisions.	Analytical- observant, probing, gather comparable information, benchmarking, propose solutions.	Managing senior level constituent / customer relations to provide world class customer service.

Potential Companies

Integrate SWOT Analysis into the Process

As previously mentioned, it is imperative to differentiate yourself. One way to do this is by being more prepared than any other job candidate. According to Wikipedia, a SWOT Analysis is:

"…a structured planning method used to evaluate the Strengths, Weaknesses, Opportunities, and Threats involved in a project or in a business venture. A SWOT analysis can be carried out for a product, place, industry or person. It involves specifying the objective of the business venture or project and identifying the internal and external factors that are favorable and unfavorable to achieving that objective."

SWOT Analysis is most often credited to Albert Humphrey, who led the work through the 1960s and 1970s based on data from Fortune 500 companies. The following is a high level description of the characteristics of each of the main components:

- Strengths: What are the differentiating factors that are advantageous to the proposal?
- Weaknesses: What are factors that are a disadvantage relative to the team, process, business, or product?
- Opportunities: What features could be exploited to the advantage of the team or product? This is often related to controllable and internal to the company.
- Threats: What external factors, often outside of the control of the team, business, process, and project that can be a concern?

I started integrating SWOT analysis by creating four blocks on one sheet of paper and brainstorming specifics related to the company role for which I was applying. One of the main reasons was to see if it would be a position I would like, a position I could succeed in, and a position where I could have an immediate impact.

When I first talk with people about SWOT analysis, they think it's a fancy way of kissing up. Actually, the primary goal for me when doing the analysis was not to benefit the people I was potentially interviewing with; I needed to believe I was a good fit for a role before I could have a genuine conversation convincing someone else that I was the right fit. The SWOT analysis became a tool to allowing me to do that. If the secondary goal is to show your work and how you prepared for the interview, it can only help in the goal to differentiate yourself.

I defined each block so I stayed focused and consistent within its context. Since SWOT analysis was originally created for project settings, it's important to understand how it can be used effectively in the job-search process with a little modification and clarity.

- The *strengths* represent the skills you can bring.
- The *weaknesses* are specific to the role, the department, or even the company, based on your insight gathered from interview preparation, from articles, current/past employers, and other factors.
- The *opportunities* should be a direct reflection of the action you can take to address the weaknesses (internally focused).
- The *threats* are more externally focused and most of the time are out of your control. For example, could new federal regulations create issues in the industry you're looking to get into?

Historically, the SWOT has had great results for me by ensuring that I was fully prepared for any interview and knew that the job was definitely something I wanted. In some cases, when asked how I prepared for the interview, I might mention the SWOT analysis I completed. On more than one occasion, the interview became focused around the SWOT work itself. When that happened, I knew I had the advantage by discussing a document that I had put together, and in many cases, took some control over the flow of the interview. Although you should never manipulate an interview, having some control to play to your strengths can be the extra advantage you're looking for.

50 Institute Multi-Generation Plans into the Process

Similar to the SWOT Analysis, the multi-generation plan takes the brainstormed strategic ideas from the SWOT analysis and turns them into tactical ideas. We are often asked in interviews, "What would you do on day one?" The multi-generation plan answers what you will do on Day 30, Day 60, and Day 90 (example below).

I like to create a simple grid with columns labeled 30 Days, 60 Days, and 90 Days. The rows along the left side can be labeled and organized any way that you want. My favorite labeling method usually revolves around how I would address needs specific to *people, process, and technology* in my new role, while more technical roles are better suited to use the DMAIC methodology from process design in the category column (e.g., design, measure, analyze, improve, and control). Again, you're invited to use what works best for your particular situation.

More than once during the job search process, a hiring manager was impressed with the plan and actually used it—even when I wasn't hired. The plan leaves a lasting impression and differentiates you. I don't always share it unless it naturally fits into the conversation. My goal for doing this work is related to being prepared, and having a literal plan of attack for when I get hired. On my first day of work with my new employer, I was able to turn my multi-generation plan into a task list, and hit the ground running. Please note that due to the length of time to complete, it's recommended to be selective in the use of this tool. However, it is highly suggested for use with the best leads.

Multi-Generation Plan Example

Category	30 Days	60 Days	90 Days +
People			
Process			
Technology			

Track Everything

Be organized. You should track every move you make to help facilitate the tactics needed to land the big job. Every job description you apply for should go into a folder (paper or online depending on your style), while every piece of contact information gathered via LinkedIn, email, etc., should go into your contact repository. Beside it, include a potential action to call, send an email, check out their webpage, or read their LinkedIn profile, for example. You never know when you will use it or need it. It's a good idea to create a tracking sheet that includes who you contacted, the date of actions taken with the outcome, and follow-up date with next steps. I liked to transfer my written notes to a central reference location to keep everything in one place for summary purposes and for efficiency with my next steps.

Job-seeking Tracking Sheet Example:

Contact Name	Company	Contact Made (email, phone)	Date	Next Follow-Up Date	Follow-up Action	Comments

Avoid Supportive Words

It's important to stay away from descriptions on your résumé that simply show you were along for the ride with respect to job responsibilities. For example, *supported* and *assisted* don't show your leadership skills. Avoid words that make it sound like you simply did what was asked of you. Although that's a good trait, it's also expected. It's important to use strong and active words that clearly define the type of work that you executed. For example, *enhanced, exceeded, formulated, generated, implemented, increased,* and *influenced* are just a few power words that grab the reader's attention. The list can go on forever. The Internet and a thesaurus are great resources to find strong, active words that can help shape your résumé. If you are applying at larger organizations or online, there is a high likelihood that your résumé *and* cover letter are being scanned for many of these key words. Even though I've stressed being unique and differentiating yourself, some conformity is important to ensure that your résumé stands out.

53 Have Your Résumé Tell Your Story

Your résumé should tell *your story* based on *your* set of experiences. Although you must manipulate your résumé to match the job requirements, it's important that *you* feel good about the product you're putting in front of people. One version of my résumé was described as "wordy," which was an accurate assessment. I did need to cut it down, but I was still judicious enough to know that it might be scanned and run through algorithms that would be picked up online. I took some chances in assuming that those formulas were looking for specific words, not word counts. The reason I noted that I still needed to reduce the total number of words is because, anecdotally, most people give your résumé no more than a thirty-second look. An economy of well-thought-out words became important over time—but it had to be done within my own story framework.

As for my story, I was told to remove a "Personal" section from the bottom. I know that interviewers aren't allowed to ask personal questions, such as, "How many children do you have?", unless it's relevant to a specific job. My "Personal" section included, "Married with three children… Excellent health; runs 20+ miles per week…Published Two Books." In a split second, a reviewer will know that I'm stable (on paper at least), won't miss work, and probably know how to communicate effectively. Although a pessimist may say that you will miss work because of sick children or school obligations, I was willing to show pride in my family and courage to be just a little different. In the many years I've asked training groups and experts what they thought when they read it, it was very rare that anyone saw anything but positive signs. I chose to keep it because it distinguished me from the crowds and was *my story*. Remember: sameness and conformity are not okay unless you have a reason for them.

54 Do Your Homework

In addition to SWOT Analysis and multi-generation plans, it's imperative that you do your homework prior to meeting with people from any company—even if it's not an interview. Homework goes far beyond a company's website. Doing your homework includes using LinkedIn individual profiles prior to networking sessions and engaging in group discussions on pertinent subject matter. Just because it's not an interview doesn't mean you can go in and wing it. You need to be ready to be engaged in a dialog rather than simply begging for a job. During a networking session, I once asked the individual how to get actual interviews with some of her peers whom I had already networked with in the past. Her response was, "You already had the interview when you networked." That was a powerful statement that has remained with me: every conversation is a potential interview.

If you are fortunate enough to get an official interview, you must start digging in even further to gather more information. You can start by going on the company website—the operative word is *start*. In your effort to be seen as unique among the masses, understand that going on the website is what everyone else does, too. It's important to understand the company's mission and culture, but that is only surface information. How do the mission and culture come alive? Who do you know working there or who previously worked there? Do you have anyone in your Facebook or LinkedIn contacts? Can you look at current employee or alumni groups on LinkedIn, looking for people you may know or can connect with prior to the interview? Do you know people at a career center who may have contacts? Look for HR connections though LinkedIn or group discussions. If you have Twitter, look for how the company is sending out their regular messaging. Look for news features or articles about the company to get a holistic view. It's vital to do more than read the company's mission statement.

Homework may also include role playing, mock interviewing, or bouncing ideas off your mentors in preparation for job interviews and networking. You can read the "Practice Interviewing" chapter for more tips.

Know Your Audience

As part of your homework, it's critical that you know with whom you are talking—not just his or her name and title. Do you know their interests, their past roles, their accomplishments? If it's not an interview but a networking session, it may be a slightly different conversation since you're not restricted to protocol about interview boundaries. I wouldn't recommend being too casual, but I suggest being more creative in your approach about topics to discuss.

I suggest keeping things professional; however, you do have more latitude to talk about potential common interests and connection points. For example, you can talk about running marathons or how many kids he or she may have in their family, when it makes sense. Conversely, try to understand what topics are taboo. I once asked a contact how his wife was doing, as I knew the couple when they used to live nearby. He mentioned their recent divorce. I couldn't have gotten every bit of information in advance to ensure the conversation went smoothly, but I could have been more attentive to the fact that he was only talking about his kids, and not pressed the question about his spouse unless it came up more naturally. It made the discussion awkward for a little bit. We recovered, but it was a good lesson in the importance of a better awareness of the surroundings and situations. As much as personal connections will enhance the relationship, I've learned to do enough homework to be sure, allow others to bring subjects up first, or to stay away from personal topics until a deeper relationship is forged.

What do you know about the audience with whom you're interviewing? Look for more than personal facts, especially in an interview, since the dynamics are slightly different from a pure networking session. Do you know the person's style and personality type? Does the person you're interviewing with like humor? Are they "down-to-earth;" are they shirt-and-tie-type where everything stays extremely professional; are they looking for past history or go-forward dialog? Stay true to yourself in the interview but when you know how to adapt, it can be a key factor to making the most of the conversation.

56 Know Your Communication and Leadership Capabilities

According to the August 2013 article "When Clubs Mean Business" by Jennifer L. Blanck in *Toastmaster Magazine*, "Communication and leadership skills ranked at the top of employers' list of attributes desired in new hires, in both 2011 and 2012 Corporate Recruiters Survey." This is consistent with many other studies that show the importance of communicating, influencing, and inspiring. Go back and read some of your past performance appraisals and talk with past managers, friends, and colleagues, to learn which specific skills you have and which ones you need to refine. Strong communication and leadership skills are a requirement to not only land most jobs, but to succeed in them. When you can prove that you can do both, companies will be willing to pay for these skills.

"Why should we hire you?" This standard question often throws off too many people. Simply saying that you have these skills out loud won't get you very far. Many people already know the importance of these skills and will say, "I'm a great communicator and leader." However, what is that person really saying? It's hard to tell. When you go down this route, you must provide tangible examples of both. More importantly, it's important to clearly articulate what value you will add to the company. Do you truly understand your unique value? How can you distinguish yourself? In addition to the experiences that may help, what is your expertise?

I liked to provide examples of instances when I showed extreme flexibility, cleaned up some messes, or started up brand new pieces of the business. I will caution you of the dangers of living in the past only. To be effective, you should be able to take these past experiences and translate them into your future—how you will make the *new* business better. Your SWOT, multi-generation plan, and more importantly, your differentiating story, can start to come alive with specific context. That is the value proposition.

57 Evaluate Your Finite Time

According to discussions with several career centers, consultants, and recruiters, I've heard that networking directly contributed to hiring by as much as 85 percent. I believe it. Are you spending the majority of your time putting in as many applications as possible, roaming websites, or establishing networking sessions? Are you spending the right amount of time with the right people? I want to continue to emphasize the need to keep all options open, but it's also important to evaluate your time and prioritize how you choose to spend it.

I was invited to a local networking group about an hour away—in Maine, everything is considered local based on how spread out the state is. I strongly considered going until I compared the amount of time to get there and aligned the types of business people who would be there compared to my goals. Most of the attendees would be owners of small businesses. As much as I am a supporter of small business, my immediate goals would have been sacrificed each week for several hours to attend. I couldn't afford to give up prime contact hours. I don't want to contradict my emphasis on casting a broad net, but we can only throw it so far when there are only twenty-four hours in a day. I chose to reprioritize my time around these prime hours. There are a growing number of professional groups that are phenomenal in getting people together to share stories and provide opportunities. This particular one didn't work out for me, but I was able to attend several others at libraries and career centers that were productive for me as one-time shots. It's important to regularly evaluate whether something is moving you forward toward your goals. The value may change over time, as well, so be sure to reevaluate as time goes on.

58 Call in Favors

If now isn't a good time to call in some favors, when is? We never want to be indebted to anyone, and we should always be thinking about reciprocity. Personally I don't keep score as to who owes me. However, there are helpful people you know, and some you haven't even met yet, who are secondary contacts who will welcome the opportunity to assist you in any way. My wife always says that "Things always equal out in the end," whether it's finding a quarter or losing one. If someone *owes you*, you wouldn't want him or her to feel obligated to reciprocate, but I do feel confident that I've surrounded myself with many people who would anyway. The key message is to not be afraid to call in a favor.

Keep Moving

Get Over It

I was told by a friend that "It's okay to be angry." My internal response was, "At who? For what?" My former company made a budget decision. It's the cost of doing business. I confirmed it had nothing to do with job performance and began to see that good could and would come out of the situation. I could have screamed or punched a wall. I guess I realized early on that logic and action would get me to my next goal. I chose to pursue my goals with action and not waste unnecessary energy on *What Could Have Been* scenarios. Your work identity with your old company ended on the day that you left. Now is the time to pursue the next stage in your life. I only recall one truly bad day where I felt that nothing was going right, as you may recall from the headhunter chapter. You'll find out about the day when I genuinely understood how headhunters worked in an upcoming chapter.

Even looking back on the sea of red-colored Microsoft Excel spreadsheet cells showing all my rejections or leads with no progress, I only saw that the next phone call or email would be the one to change the course of my life and career. If I had wasted time, someone else may have been landing my job. I chose to attack the situation with a strong work ethic—my job was to look for a job. I was working for myself and for my family and I wanted to succeed—I had to get over it. It was not unusual for me to put in ten to twelve hour days looking for my next job, knowing that the payoff would be worth it.

60   Stay Healthy

It's easy to feel sorry for yourself or even be too dedicated in the job search to think about your health. It is critical to maintain a healthy life style by exercising and eating right. You will need the energy in your pursuit for the best job. A healthy lifestyle also helps to keep the cobwebs out of your head and allows you to see the path ahead more clearly. The exercising was also a time to reflect on what was happening, or, sometimes, to allow for a quick disconnect from the job search. Even if you didn't exercise or eat right before, now is the time to start. The message isn't intended to be preachy, but the unknown of how long the process will take, the reality of staring at a computer screen for hours, and the mental toll of constant rejection can take a lot out of you. I'm not sure I can say that I bounded out of bed each day, but I can say that I attacked each day with vigor.

# Be Open and Honest About the Situation

You can't hide from the facts. Yes, you've lost your job, but you didn't lose your identity. You might feel the need to hold back on information, but being open, and even vulnerable, isn't a bad trait when people are trying to help. If you have kids, the age of the children will dictate how much filtering is needed in your messaging to them. My kids were twelve, fourteen, and sixteen years old when I had to tell them about the job loss. My wife and I were straightforward and simple with our approach. I said that I lost my job due to budget cuts, but had the utmost confidence that I would land a job as soon as I could. I emphasized that my job was to find a job and that *each day was a work day.*

We found that that matter of fact approach reduced the burden that children sometimes feel they have to carry. Holding back because of embarrassment or other reasons will only cause more mental anguish as you try to bottle up. Make the effort to be more open with the information. You'll find a very large population of people who have been through it, who know someone who has gone through it, or are simply there to help. The support comes when people start to know your story.

62 Enjoy the Rollercoaster

Don't feel sorry for yourself. First, you don't have time and second, it is your choice as to how you will resolve this situation. You can choose to feel down in the dumps, or you can go after the new challenge with gusto. It's okay to feel excited about the unknown test that is staring you in the face. You should enjoy the ride—because at this point, it's the only ride you're on. It may seem masochistic to relish this type of situation, but I realized how important maintaining the right attitude was to my success in this endeavor. Enjoy the rollercoaster ride of emotions as doors open and shut all around you. In Dr. Richard Carlson's book *Don't Sweat the Small Stuff* he notes, "Don't let the highs be too high and the lows be too low." Stay balanced with your approach, and you will win the game.

Continue to Help Others

You are bound to run into other unemployed people. In fact, a close friend of mine was looking for a job at the same time. I could have said we were *competing* for openings, but in reality we simply shared best practices, gave each other advice, and maintained the special "unemployment bond" that brought us even closer. When we both landed jobs within a couple weeks of each other, the success was only sweeter. My two months of unemployment was full of mistakes and lessons learned. I felt a need to share this information with anyone I thought could benefit from it. I considered this invested time, while always testing my theories and getting feedback on my trials and tribulations for the future. A job may not be right for you but if someone else comes to mind, pay it forward.

In these desperate times, it sounds counterintuitive, but it's important to share your expertise and knowledge and expect nothing in return. Whether you are in a one-on-one session, talking with career centers, or speaking with professional/networking groups, you should willingly participate. You obviously don't want to come across as a know-it-all, but you will gain credibility and value naturally when people see your selfless behavior and leadership skills. When you do things because it's the right thing to do, not because you need a job, the job ends up finding you. It may take some time, but your patience and generosity will pay dividends for you over time.

64. Maintain Your Mentors

Mentors are like that blanket you couldn't give up as a kid. If you don't have to stop the relationship, then don't. Mentors provide the objective point of view we all need. If your mentor is with your old company, unless policy dictates it, there is no reason to stop the conversations. One of my mentors hit me between the eyes with some feedback as I was looking into options to get back into my former company when she said, "Tone down the outside interests." She meant that my "paid hobby" of speaking and training on the side could easily be seen as a priority conflict. Although I saw the strength of these interests as making me a stronger professional, my mentor's easily digestible comment put a potential blind spot into context. Someone who may not know me well might easily shy away from wanting to hire me due to a perceived priority conflict. I was able to work on my filtering of this information in networking and job interviews by not leading with it. I formulated a more reserved message that came across stronger because it was clear how those side interests had become an investment in my own growth that would help me succeed in the new role. I am ever so thankful for the mentors, both formal and informal, who stayed with me through this process.

Be a Mentor

What does an unemployed individual have to offer as a mentor? Plenty! In fact, I picked up more people to mentor along the way than I would have ever expected. It is always flattering to be asked. My time-management skills were challenged, forcing me to be creative in how often we met, but I am convinced that leading discussions and helping others kept me sharp and on my game. It also allowed me to question myself about whether I was being productive in my own efforts to grow and develop.

66 Find Outside Activities

You must keep up with industry trends and stay sharp. As part of my routine, I read relevant articles and paid attention to LinkedIn group discussions. In addition, I continued being an active part of Toastmasters International. Although Toastmasters may not be the solution for everyone, it kept my writing and communication skills honed and kept my confidence up with a very supportive group. It also got me out of the house. For me, it was like a play date for adults. The satisfaction level of participating in activities with a group of people with similar goals was very motivating. Additionally, I kept a journal containing all the lessons I learned during the job search process. That journal became the basis of this book. It's important to balance your job search with professional development. Make sure you read books, websites, and keep your network productive. It all leads to the same place, and the invested time may be the differentiating factor when it comes to preparation, knowledge, and relevant skills.

Know What You Want

Not this again! Yes, this again, but with a different spin. A motivational speaker by the name of Lewis Timberlake mentioned this almost fifteen years ago when I saw him, and I never forgot it.

- Know what you want.
- Know that you deserve it.
- Know what you're giving up to get it.

The third bullet always grabs me, because many of us often feel we deserve so much more than we have or get. The question is, "What are you willing to give up to get it?" Are you willing to travel more than you ever have? Are you willing to see your family less? Are you willing to work from home? Are you willing to take a pay cut to get your foot in the door? Are you willing to shift other priorities? Are you willing to work eighty-hour work weeks? The questions can go on and on. We may get a high paying job, but are you getting the other things in return, such as job satisfaction? Know *exactly* what you want.

68 Be True to You

With so many supporters dispensing advice, it's easy to get caught up, especially when some of it can be contradictory. My advice is to take it all. Similar to the chapter, "Know That Your Résumé Is Yours," when you're going through the process of finding a job, be willing to grow while staying true to you. What's most important to you? What is non-negotiable? In the swirl of the job search, you may not feel you have too much say or control over what is negotiable—but you do. As stated in the excerpt of the speech in the introduction to this book, my oldest daughter told me that relocating wasn't an option. I set deadlines for myself in the job search process. In the first few months, relocation wasn't an option. It was non-negotiable. I had in my mind that if there were no real leads, then I would make adjustments to this goal. Time changes goals, so keep them fluid, but it's important to balance what's right for you and whoever else is impacted. I suggest staying firm to what you want and who you really want to be. You don't have to settle or compromise unless new facts come that may change your direction. Go back to the chapter, "Answer the Critical Questions" and determine *your* specifics relating to location, satisfaction, and compensation, to ensure you are true to yourself.

 **Turn Your Passions into Your Career**

One of my favorite quotes, "Opportunity seldom labels itself," is credited to an unknown author. A number of mentors and people within the network suggested I take my side interests of speaking, training, and coaching and make them a full-time endeavor. As appetizing as that sounded, I still felt a passion to go back to the banking industry. With the down-turned economy, the banking industry has been beaten up. The industry has been wounded, but there are far too many opportunities in the risk avoidance space to turn away from it altogether. I'm passionate about fixing problems and have a strong history of start-up roles. The job I was ultimately offered and accepted was brand new, and fit both categories. Even with so many unknowns, what you do know are your passions. Run toward them. To paraphrase Steve Cohen, professor of public speaking, and one who had to go through a similar process in his own past, "Be inspired to look to leverage your passions to make money."

70 Break Out of Your Comfort Zone

It's hard to tell you to look outside your previous industry when I landed a job in the same industry I'd been in for over twenty years. It's logical to go toward your comfort zone, and it's a lot easier to demonstrate your strengths in order to land the job. However, when I say I cast a broad net, I truly did. I looked into expanding my own business. I looked into professional training firms, health care, sales, marketing, and many other avenues. You will start to understand there is more out there than the fences you remain confined within. After you've broadened your scope to explore other fields, then you can consider it a well-thought-out plan, even if you choose to stay within your field in the end.

71   Take a Different Route

Returning to the theme of differentiating yourself, I found when I was meeting with professional groups, career center clients, etc., that I was surrounded by people who were just like me—they were unemployed. As obvious as this may sound, my next thought was that they couldn't help me, or in some cases, they could actually be competing with me. What I found was the opposite—we were all in this together. The amount of anger, fear, apprehension, confusion and many other feelings varied from individual to individual, but we found solace in our shared predicament. Our support groups sitting around talking about our problems made others in the group open up. As people opened up, others began to offer suggestions. "I know someone who used to work there," or "Let me introduce you to someone I know who may be able to help you," were common comments.

It became important in these group settings to clearly direct the dialog in a way that had each individual focusing on what they wanted and needed to move forward in their pursuit of a job, not just on the emotional rollercoaster ride we were all on. In some cases, we asked specifically if there was anyone in the room who had a contact or connections specific to what an individual member wanted or needed. Although it began slowly, that networking process became contagious as members realized we all had some loose connections and expertise that others could benefit from. I didn't realize we were practicing a concept that Adam Grant discusses in his book *Give and Take* as a "Reciprocity Ring." Becoming aware of that concept helped me to further and more explicitly drive the conversation down the path of action.

Note: for those wondering where to start to find professional groups and networking groups, there are many ways to begin your search. I suggest you start local. You can check with your local chamber of commerce, ask people during your individual networking sessions, look on social media sites (e.g., Facebook, LinkedIn), and check out career centers and libraries.

72 Live for the Future

My job identity with my past employer was lost as soon as I walked out the door. I had plenty of accolades and accomplishments to be proud of. However, I couldn't live in the past. I needed to move toward the future. Have you ever been a part of a conversation that began, "When I was with (insert company name here)…"? It's always good to share best practices and give people the confidence that you have the right experience to do a job well, but it can grow tiresome for your audience. For a more meaningful, productive conversation, articulate how past experiences relate to what you can bring to the new company going forward.

Think of the phrase, "What have you done for me lately?" Every prospective employer wants to know your value proposition. When talking about the impact you can have, or even when beginning a new position, ask, "How is it done?" and then follow that up with, "How well is that process working? Are there improvements that will make it work better?" You can offer potential solutions without mentioning your prior company. Don't be the person who identifies themselves too often with their past company. Your identity should be much more related to your competencies and experience. Without mentioning the former company name, you can still mention, "Has the company thought about or tried any of the following solutions…?" Formulating immediate and long-term ideas for the kind of impact you can have on the new company will go a long way and produce something more effective than, "That's the way it used to be."

73. Don't Accept No News as Good News

Early in the job search process, I tried to convince myself when I made it through the final interviews that no news was good news—rationalizing that my prospective employer had to inform the other candidates that they weren't being hired before making me an offer. It didn't take long to realize that I was kidding myself. As previously mentioned about follow-up, if the date I was given for a callback passed or I wasn't given a date and an unusually long period of time had gone by with no contact, I made a call or sent a note to keep the process moving and try to remain relevant. In some of my more hopeful leads, I found too much silence—no returned messages—when I attempted to contact the decision-makers. In some cases, there really were no answers to give, since we all know that business is constantly changing. Organizational changes can easily cause delays or alter the original thoughts about the opening. Unfortunately, I found a couple of occasions when individuals were delaying the inevitable of giving me the bad news. Personally, if I'm going to get bad news, I'd rather have it as soon as possible so I know the best next steps to take. I remained professionally persistent, and requested full transparency when it came to better knowing the facts and determining what I needed to do for a better response the next time something similar became open.

74

Vent Out Loud

Although I genuinely felt no sustained anger for the business decision that was made to eliminate my job, and I feel the number of good days far outweighed the number of bad days, there were inevitably moments when I wanted to scream... So I did. Whether it's finding a trusted advisor or family member to talk to or simply sticking your tongue out at the laptop screen, we all need a way to get past whatever is causing the frustration. It's important to release it, and then refocus the energy back to the task at hand. Don't just swim in the middle of the frustration and hope it goes away; it will only linger. Address it head on, and then move forward.

75 Lean on Your Support Group

Whether your support group is one person or many, an organized group, an impromptu gathering, or a phone call, family, friends, or even a mentor, find a way to assess your needs and lean on this group for solutions. A support group is different from your network in the sense that your dependence on them truly is for support. You must actively seek out support for your own sanity. Having an objective point of view from someone who's not so deep into the process will provide you valuable insight. You can be productive by bouncing new ideas, troubleshooting actions that may not be working, or brainstorming new ones. It is impossible to do all of this on your own.

Know Where Your Eggs Are

Are all of your eggs in the same basket? Were you panicked because your entire network was from the same company, or worse, from your building location? Not everyone is in the same position when it comes to building a network. Some networks are more mature than others, and connecting with people who immediately surround you at work is a good start. However, your ability to expand beyond your existing company will open up more opportunities for you. For example, are you part of any professional groups or clubs such as Rotary, Lions or Kiwanis? Are your kids in school, sports, or clubs? I found this opened up a significant amount of doors by giving me the chance to meet other children's parents. Your employer provides great opportunities to build your network, but that should be a building block and not the only way that you meet people and network. It's time to fly out of the nest and broaden your horizons. Recognize that networking opportunities surround you, and be open to tapping into them.

77 Fight Feelings of Isolation

As isolated as we may feel in this sea of angst, we have a support system. The support can come from your immediate family, your extended family, your old friends, new friends you meet along the way, your social network, and your business network. It is not possible to do it alone. As much as you may feel alone in the process, it is critical to lean on the people around you for support, for a shoulder to cry on, for the push you need but may not want. Your success is dependent on the people around you. Statistically, the analysis will tell you that networking is the main reason for successful job searches. Even for a little bit of sanity during the process, you can use the people around you to help you think more clearly or to be the wall to throw something at to see if it sticks. As much as you may feel alone in the process, you are not—just ask my running partner, Kevin. Okay, he's not a person, he's a dog, but the morning jogs with him were just as much for clearing my head as they were for physical wellness.

Maximize Your Soft and Hard Skills

78 Be Detailed and Succinct

As an interviewer, I once sat back for twenty minutes and waited for a candidate to finish answering the first question of the interview, "Tell me a little bit about yourself professionally." The answer was rambling and meandered all around with no particular end in sight. I could have stopped him, but part of the interview was to determine how effectively an individual could communicate with others. When in an interview, it's important to provide an answer that has context to the question, supported with a strong example, than a quick wrap up and conclusion. Rambling creates questions in the interviewer's mind about your overall communication style, skills, and ability. You obviously don't want one-word responses, but you do want to use solid and supporting examples using an economy of words.

As I teach in *From Fear to Success: A Practical Public-speaking Guide*, there can never be too much practice and preparation, whether you are doing mock interviews or practicing in front of a mirror using any one of the thousands of "typical" interview questions you can find on the Internet. It's not about memorization—it's about using an economy of words that hits the interviewer between the eyes with an unforgettable impact. Pull out a list of ten to twenty questions, write out your answers, and practice speaking them. The self-assessment on whether you are babbling or hitting the mark can make a huge difference in being invited back for more interviews, or even offered the job.

79

Listen Intently

Effective listening skills will get you far in the interviewing process. Interviewing is a two-way dialog, not just a question and answer session. The discussion goes both ways. However, many times candidates feel the need to talk as much about themselves as possible, as quickly as possible, in order to make sure they fit everything within the interview timeframe. It's good to be able to confidently talk about yourself (e.g., "It's Not Bragging if It's a Fact"), but the overall quantity must be carefully thought out. Unfortunately, I fell into this trap in one of my interviews.

In doing my homework for a position, I learned that the hiring manager was concerned that, although I was a leader of many tasks specific to the role for which I was interviewing, she wanted examples of when I'd rolled up my sleeves and actually done the job. I was prepared with multiple examples, and tried to find a way to include them all—and I mean *all*. I needed to better listen to the questions, stay succinct, and remain on task with my answers. I overwhelmed the interviewer and spent most of the time talking, and in my own view, unfairly dominating the discussion. The interviewer most likely felt that she'd lost control of the interview, that I wasn't engaged, and that I was simply sticking to my own agenda. Listening skills are critical to ensure that both parties get the most out of the dialog. Ironically, I went back to my handwritten notes and noticed insider information that I needed to remember: "(Hiring manager) likes to talk."

 **Don't Be Shy with Your Résumé**

Without shoving my résumé and marketing plan down everyone's throat, I wasn't shy about including it in emails and handing it out as much as possible—when it made sense. In addition to attaching it to every networking invitation, I made it part of my daily routine to create an online profile with companies I was interested in, and also uploaded it to career-assistance websites. These types of opportunities surround us if we look hard enough. For example, I found a strong information source with Career Management Associates. CMA is an HR consulting firm for Northern New England (www.cmacareer.com). Although more jobs will come from networking connections, there are opportunities locally, regionally, and nationally where companies and recruiters actively scan these types of websites. What could it hurt?

Another reason for getting the résumé out there is an objective opinion. Being unemployed had me staring at my résumé for what seemed like hours each day. As your résumé is being circulated, people will inevitably provide unsolicited advice (or solicited if we're smart enough to ask). Some of the better pieces of feedback came from these objective observers. A second set of eyes can also pick up on any typos. If you are adjusting the résumé along the way—as you should in order to target positions with your competencies—you may miss a crucial edit. What always seems like a simple, quick change has a tendency to go unnoticed until the most inopportune time.

Think About Consulting and Contracting

If you have a significant amount of expertise in a certain field, there are plenty of opportunities to contract and consult. There are pros and cons. The consultant or independent contractor is typically paid better, because companies don't have the extra expense of health benefit costs and they have a clear ending deadline, paying only for actual work being done. For both parties, it can become a trial for potential full-time work. On the down side, as a contractor you must always be concerned with the length of your contract, and try to stay ahead of when the next potential contract may come. Additionally, contractors often put in a lot of work in a condensed period of time. However, you get the higher pay and have an independent and entrepreneurial approach to getting the work done. At the very least, it can bridge the gap between full-time jobs. It is worth an individual assessment to see if it can work for you.

82   Find a Good Editor of Your Work

Spell check doesn't count as editing—just ask any *manger [sic]* or, on one of my résumé examples, where I wrote *business* singular when I meant it to be plural *businesses*. There are some techniques to tighten up the process, which include waiting until the day after writing to proofread, printing something out, reading it backwards, and reading it aloud. What you must remember is that your mind substitutes missing and wrong letters and words naturally for you. As much as we may convince ourselves that we can do it on our own, you should not proofread your own work.

Be Bold

Now is not the time to hold back. Be intellectually curious. Ask questions to move conversations along, ask questions to broaden your knowledge base, ask questions about the people you're meeting. As a naturally shy individual, this concept does not come easily to me. I learned to break out of my comfort zone for a couple of obvious reasons. First, I was fully accountable to initiate enough actions to find myself a job, and couldn't sit idly by waiting for opportunities and answers to come to me. Second, what did I have to lose? I stretched myself further outside my comfort zone than I ever had, and continued to remain self-confident. In my line of questioning, I made sure to not be so assertive that it turned people away. The goal was to build relationships. I did, however, want people to know what I was looking for, made sure to ask the right questions to move down a productive path, and ensured that there were no assumptions left on the table.

84 Practice Interviewing

When teaching how to interview effectively, I emphasize the need to practice, or mock interview. Here are the keys to make the most of the experience:

- Don't let the word "mock" throw you off—treat it as a real interview and maximize the experience. Real practice turns into real success.
- Set it up now—it's best to do it before you need it, but if that time has passed, still set them up before the next *big* interview is on the horizon.
- Make it a regular event, not a one-time shot—cramming becomes obvious. Mock interviews are practice, thus need to be done more than once.
- Understand it is a learning experience—be willing to make mistakes.
- Meet with multiple people with different styles. Talk with someone you do not know well.
- If you are currently employed, use your manager in the process, but understand that he or she does not count as a mock interview. I've found that when I worked with managers, the questions tended to be slanted to my strengths or weaknesses, which took away from the feel of a real interview. Broaden your scope to find the most effective interview partner.
- Use the exercise as a networking opportunity or a way to get your foot in a door that might otherwise be closed.

It's important to understand what mock interviews are not:

- An attempt to kiss up
- An attempt to predict questions
- An attempt to articulate answers you think the interviewer wants to hear
- A working session or brainstorming session focusing on your strengths and weaknesses—this should be done far ahead of a mock interview.

Understanding the power of mock interviews ensures that you are more comfortable in pressure situations, and keeps you sharp for the day when you need to make the intended impression.

Prepare Your Elevator Speech

If you got on an elevator and only had two floors to impress the CEO with who you are and what you've accomplished, could you do it? Before you think this is hypothetical, let me tell you the story of a former colleague who actually had this happen. We both were in town for a business meeting and were working out in the hotel fitness center early in the morning. We also saw my former company's CEO working out every day that week, but we had no interaction. I had an early flight Friday morning, but my friend went to work out again. When he was done exercising, he was just walking onto the elevator when the CEO stuck his hand in to keep the doors open so he could enter.

An interview is a similar situation, when you're under pressure and only have a finite amount of time to influence and impact the conversation. If someone says, "Tell me about yourself professionally," are you ready? Will your answer take two minutes? Ten? Fifteen? Can you adapt it to meet the needs of the interviewer or person with whom you're networking, so that your past translates into solving that specific company's business challenges? An elevator speech hits the high notes both personally and professionally. How much you incorporate in relating your personal answer depends on the circumstances and the person with whom you're speaking. However, on the professional front, your elevator speech should be a clearly laid out map relating to your recent work, your key accomplishments, and your future goals. I recommend writing out a two-minute version and a five-to-ten minute version, and then know both versions inside and out. Be careful to remember that this is not a script; you can deviate as needed. The pitch should be a base to begin a *confident* discussion. Having a foundation will allow you to modify your elevator speech as needed. If you don't know yourself inside and out, then who will? More importantly, it goes beyond just knowing—you must be able to clearly articulate it. If you can't confidently tell your own story, what kind of impression are you leaving?

Know that Every Interview is a Great Interview

In the middle of a real interview, the HR Director says to me, "Stop the BS and stop with the buzzwords. What do you really want?" So, this interview must have been going well. Based on what I had learned while preparing for the interview, it became obvious before I even walked in the door that my background and style wouldn't fit well with this company. However, I wanted to keep it moving in case my assumptions were wrong, or at least get in the practice of interviewing.

I knew less than five minutes into the questioning that I would not be hired. Instead of loafing through the rest of the interview, I made a conscious effort to make the most of the experience. I challenged myself to adapt to the interviewer's style. I pushed myself out of my comfort zone by trying to be even more creative than usual with my answers and tested various versions of my elevator speech. My goal was to see what could potentially work and what might not. Why not? What did I have to lose? I loved the challenge of the uphill battle. I even saw enough pause in some of the HR director's questions and answers to indicate that she was considering changing her mind—not enough to hire me, but enough for me to walk out of there happy that I had gone through with it. If your interview is not going well, you can use the experience as practice for future sessions. What could have been a terrible interview turned out great—at least in my eyes, which was a confidence boost.

Recognize Varying Priorities

My number one priority was to find a job. As the book title says, my job was to look for a job. It is hard not to get frustrated when people you've networked with or sought assistance from don't return calls and messages within your timeframe, but a colleague of mine put it in perspective for me: "When you're done talking with them, they go back to their job." As painful as it was to hear at the time, she was right that my priorities may not have directly aligned with those of everyone with whom I was speaking. My goal shouldn't have been to change their priorities to match mine. The goal should always be to keep the process flowing and build a relationship strong enough that it can be further developed over time.

When setting up networking sessions, if you are waiting for something from someone, gently nudge things along with a reminder. If someone requests a reminder, give it. In fact, be proactive enough to ask if it's okay to follow up if you don't hear from someone after a certain deadline. You must maintain your own priorities, but be conscious that they may not match someone else's primary focus. Understand that after you hang up the phone, your network contact goes back to work. Don't take it personally, but do take the steps necessary to remain professionally relevant.

 **Go Beyond Skills, Experience, Talent, and Tenure**

After so many years in the same job, we feel entitled to things like more vacation time, higher pay, and opportunities for promotions. If you're looking for a job, that all goes out the window. Skills, experience, talent, expertise, and tenure may no longer be enough. Do you know what companies are looking for? Is the make-up of a corporate culture *young and hip?* Are they looking for independent thinkers who are *creative and innovative?* You may not be able to put all of the weight you want on a certain skill set you possess, your years of experience, or your specific expertise. All of these components may support a way to differentiate yourself, but they could also be a hindrance if you put all of your stock into saying that your résumé will sell everything for you. Today's environment is constantly evolving, and certain organizations may be looking for traits that go beyond experience level or past years doing a particular job. The important thing to remember is not to be surprised when this happens. What's vital is that you understand how to deepen your own thinking to align yourself to the creative thinking of the culture of the organizations you want to be a part of. Once you start to work with it, you will become more nimble in your job-seeking and networking discussions.

Keep the Lines of Communication Open

It's important to keep in regular touch with your network, whether it is through social media channels, email, or other means. You can provide status updates, share information that you've read (e.g., articles), or simply thank individuals or groups for their support and assistance. Similar to social media, you want your *posts (emails, and others)* to be read, relevant, and considered high content. Social media is most effective when people are given something decent to read or their attention is captured—which means you can stay away from posting what you had for dinner last night. Once a story gains momentum, its popularity increases exponentially; as a result, that story is then shared. On Facebook for example, the stories that have the most comments and "likes" continue to appear in the top of the news feed for those who sort by the "most popular" criteria. I want you to think about having your content "liked." I'm not making the point to copy everyone on an email, reply all, or make it a daily event unless you have something important to communicate. What I'm emphasizing is the need to be the driver of information and to stay visible in the eyes of the people who can most help you achieve your goals. It's important to keep the lines of communication open and constant—even when you gained everything you needed from the initial conversation.

An easy way to do this is by showing your appreciation for the support you're getting. Back to the social media example, it's essential to go beyond a simple "thanks" email or post. Express to the person why you feel grateful for their efforts. If possible, if there are other people who would want or need to know what that person did for you, then copy or share with them as well. When the note becomes about them, you start to make an impact on deepening the relationship. Another way is to continue to turn the discussion around to the people with whom you're networking. I've surprised a few people when I turned the conversation around and offered my assistance by asking, "What can I do for you?" A humble approach to genuinely say *thank you* while offering your skills and services can be placed in his or her back pocket for later, and will go a long way in deepening your relationship.

Build and Maintain Your Personal Brand

Your personal brand and reputation were built long before your job search began. I had the fortunate opportunity of trying to build a literal brand with "Thomas Dowd Professional Development & Coaching, LLC." I made a lot of mistakes along the way. For example, the same core group of people I communicate with on social media were getting tired of the book solicitations, while other people were tired of hearing about the success I was having with Toastmasters speaking engagements. I learned early on that there is a fine line between, *"I wanted to share something that's going on with me"* and *"look at me."* I learned how critical it is that although it is my brand, it is not always about me. I needed to avoid misinterpreted one-way information sharing by ensuring that I was engaging other people in the dialog so that I could get to know them and understand their interests, wants, and needs, as well. I had to ensure that building and maintaining my brand was a two-way process. No one can simply throw his or her brand at someone and expect them to like it.

When's the last time you asked yourself what people may think of you? Being self-aware is great, but others may have their own perception of you—are the two aligned? For example, I was a fast walker down the halls early in my career because I didn't—and still don't—like to waste time. I found out I was considered by some as unapproachable because I didn't stop and chat a lot in the halls. What is your past reputation? Are people carrying that with them in their perceptions of you in a way that could impact your next career move? Landing a successful job is heavily based on the people we know, and how those people perceive us.

If you have a reputation as a hard-worker, that's a great reputation to have. Do you know what decision-makers or influencers of your next potential role think of you? This is where the two-way discussion can be important, by asking questions and clearly understanding how people view you—positive and negative. It's important to be proactive and drive this type of discussion. People do talk, and spread the message of your reputation. I even found examples when people at different companies in the same industry discussed my skill set.

You must continue to build your reputation and brand even in the midst of the job search by getting your name out there in a professional way so that people *want* to interact with you and *want you as part of their team*. You don't want to appear desperate, but you do want to make yourself significant in order to ensure that your name will come up in conversation.

It's a constant work in progress; reputations are built over time, and crushed in an instant. While engaged in conversation, you want to appear confident and useful for a hiring company without being arrogant. Conversely, if you were quiet and isolated in a previous job, you may have some work to do to play catch up. It's important to know that when you're looking for work, you are building your brand. If you had a bad reputation from your previous company, you can hope for a clean slate, but don't depend on it. If you feel you left on bad terms, do everything you can to fix it or at least lessen the impact. Again, people do talk, look for references, and research your past, whether through social media or other means. I suggest taking a long, hard look at your brand. Then, make modifications, delete unnecessary entries from your social media sites, and do what you can to have a brand that you're proud of.

91 Use Facts

"You should work for this company because I've heard…" or, "You shouldn't work for this company because…" I heard once at my former employer that a company up the road, constant competition for new hires, would tell prospective candidates that our company was going to close down in the next year or two, so it was best to apply now, while opportunities were still available. I don't know if there was any truth to that rumor, but I do know the need to corroborate stories and separate fact from fiction. The rumor mill can be a scary place on which to base an important professional decision that could impact you and your family. As you pursue potential companies, make sure you have multiple sources of information, including people who currently work there, people who used to work there, news media, and social media sources to help formulate your opinions using facts. You may not want to dismiss hearsay so quickly, but you do want to do your due diligence prior to making any rash decisions.

92 Keep in Touch

The day will come when you find *the* job. The day you've been waiting for. You're euphoric; your new work identity is being forged. Now what? Besides setting yourself up to start the new job right on day one by beginning to fulfill your multi-generation plan and SWOT analysis, you have an opportunity to express your sincere gratitude to the people who helped you along the way. I bet your network was an incredible help in landing you the new job. After the thanks are doled out, it doesn't end. The network is a living and breathing thing that must be nurtured; some relationships need to be further developed, while others should be deepened. You must keep in contact with your network. The frequency of contact depends on your needs, their needs, and the people themselves. There are still plenty of people in my network with whom I have too shallow a relationship, which needs to be addressed, while I still want to reinvent myself with older contacts. More importantly, there may be some people out there who I can help the way that others helped me.

You're deserving of a breather and a huge celebration for your hard work. As with the earlier message of jumping in immediately to get the job-search process started, it's important for the growth and strength of your network to maintain contact and not take networking time off. When done correctly, your network will blossom and continue to do work for you. Just as important, you can be the type of supportive person you wanted others to be when you were unemployed.

**Pertinent Chapters from *The Transformation of a Doubting Thomas:
Growing from a Cynic to a Professional in the Corporate World***

93. Wait Three Months…

On what I remember was one of the most frustrating days I have ever had with a boss in my career, my wife had the gall to say, "Wait three months and one of you will be hired (into another role), fired, promoted, or demoted." It was her way of giving me a lesson in patience. I had come home after another bad day with my boss. For many reasons, including differences in management styles, personalities, and personal goals, I just didn't get along with this particular boss. The thought had seriously crossed my mind to leave the company.

As I had found through my research with employee retention, most people choose to leave their manager rather than leaving the company. My wife was right. I needed to hang in there and things would change. Things did happen quickly. My hated boss was 'double' promoted into a different position. I didn't even think it was possible, but it happened. I could not have been happier for myself and for the fact that the person moved on. The new person who came in gave me a clean slate. He listened to my ideas and gave me opportunities to drive the business and grow.

We all know that promotions in companies do not always come quickly or easily. The message is not to sit around and wait for something to happen. Opportunities are few and far between before someone is tapped on the shoulder. The message of "wait three months" is also a call to action to build the relationship, even if it is damaged. Some of my most constructive conversations have come when I have directly said to someone, "I think we got off to a rough beginning. Do you mind if we start over," or "I think there is some misunderstanding between us." By making the first move in reaching out to smooth over a rough relationship, I have found that many people are receptive to at least listening. Many times, we had a good laugh together over the original situation as time went on.

The "three month" concept is a good reminder that time is always ticking forward and can work in your favor. Businesses are always changing and this concept shows that you can be part of the change. By exhibiting patience with a level head, and taking action to strengthen bonds and relationships, you will move forward to success in your overall career beyond those three months.

94   Be Impatiently Patient

Maybe I will do it tomorrow. 'It' could be anything. Tomorrow I will set my goals. Tomorrow I will earn the big promotion. Tomorrow I will write the next great novel. Some of us keep wishing and some of us allow frustration to build up. Still, we take no action, except maybe a complaint or two, or maybe three. We have all heard that good things come to those who wait. However, I will tack on that great things will come to those who earn it and take action.

I have had many career conversations with individuals who complained that his or her manager had rarely, if ever, had a career development conversation with him or her. The complaints include comments that his or her manager has performance-based conversations that help with the present, but lack the long-term discussion to push them further in their careers. I have seen consistent focus group feedback and anonymous survey feedback reiterating the same thing.

I have had to provide some tough feedback to people by asking them, "When was the last time you read your performance appraisal?" A very large percentage of people I ask have answered that it was the day it was administered. People have a silver tray of feedback on their lap that they think they can memorize after a thirty to sixty-minute discussion. They are wrong. People need to reinforce the constructive feedback that will make them better. They should not wait for the next performance review that will take place six months to a year from the last one. People should take hold of that feedback and take action immediately. Grab the feedback head on and start to implement the actions needed to make you stronger. Be impatiently patient to make yourself better.

If the complaints are accurate and you are really not getting career advice or long-term direction, you have the right to understand and ask for it. You need to know exactly what it takes to get promoted or get to the next level, or even what it takes to maintain great performance results.

The conversation does not have to be contentious or even demanding. A simple request of, "Can you help me to better understand what it takes…" can go a long way.

Everyone should do their homework to at least know the minimum requirements and expectations for their current role and what is needed to get to the next level. My former company used to have minimum requirements to get promoted to certain officer positions, including taking certain courses, and submitting at least one original, formal, creative idea annually to make the business better. I would be amazed any time I had a conversation with a colleague who said he or she could not come up with a fresh idea or find the time to take the training courses.

The irony may be that the driving force for me early in my career was my inability to take accountability. I was driven to cover my bases for all minimum requirements to ensure that never happened to me. I refused to allow any decision maker to make an easy decision to count me out of the running for an officer promotion simply because I had not met the checkbox requirements. That would make it too easy for others. Remember, I was in the habit of blaming others.

I was learning that if I was going to blame someone for not promoting me or giving me the next great role, I wanted to force the conversation to be more meaningful than, "Sorry, you missed the minimum requirements." The drive to meet the requirements forced me to be impatiently patient because I was going to meet all of my annual requirements in January (if the cycle started at the beginning of the year), as soon as I saw it in my inbox, or as soon as physically possible to complete.

My concerns for missing small details or requirements, or gaining a reputation as a procrastinator, were not part of my personality. My fear of missing a deadline or not completing my workload actually enhanced the perception of me in the eyes of many leaders. I was gaining a reputation for getting things done quickly. I was also becoming known for reading the details that may have been glossed over by others. I was building a positive reputation based on my emerging skill set.

Although others were still getting promoted around me, it was not because I wasn't meeting my goals. It was the many other components that had been reiterated many times over. My inability to change how I got the job done was holding me back (e.g., relationship building, cynicism). The positive momentum change in how I was viewed in getting things done quickly was a good sign toward future advancements.

I would eventually find my way to meeting many of my professional goals, but not within my personal, unwritten time frames. I was beginning to be more driven and more specific in establishing these goals. I would set a certain age at which I wanted to achieve a title or position. There were designated times when I wanted to expand my role. I was often close, but I was not always within my personal deadlines. I was all right with that because my impatience was driving me to take the better road to eventually get to the position or goal I wanted.

In fact, there were at least two times in my career where I was in the right place at the wrong time. I was given expanded responsibilities at a time when I was not fully prepared for the positions. In both cases, I was asked to step back to a lesser role or change my position completely. I also learned that getting exactly what you want at the wrong time can have devastating impacts professionally. I learned from both scenarios to set clear goals, but be prepared for when I get there.

The lessons of not only knowing what I wanted, but also when I wanted to get there, proved valuable. My impatience made me do more homework and research to set aggressive, but more realistic, goals. I knew myself better than anyone else and I began writing out a game plan to help me achieve my goals. Doing things on the fly and just pushing to get someplace fast happened far too many times early in my career, to my detriment. I had the drive to get there quickly, but I lacked the specificity of where I was heading. This held me back. I needed to know where I wanted to go and be impatiently patient to get there—with a plan.

Finally, if you are fortunate enough to take on a new role, you need to be impatiently patient in learning the business. You can never passively wait to meet the learning curve within a given time frame in a new position. First, you need to understand the business is moving quickly and can't wait around for you. Second, if you are effective in attacking the transition, you can accelerate your ascent to gain technical knowledge. Your patient efforts to impatiently learn the business as quickly as possible will assist you in gaining credibility with the people you are working with as you gain insights on the integration between different faces of the business, technology, culture, and styles. Take advantage of a learning curve if there is one, but learn as quickly as possible by using the people and resources around you to absorb everything.

95

Build a Network

Brian Uzzi and Shannon Dunlap tell an introductory story in their study in the Harvard Business Review article, "How to Build a Network," about the well-known Paul Revere as an historic figure in America. They then ask the question about the reader's familiarity with William Dawes. Apparently, he and Paul Revere rode from Boston on April 18, 1775 in separate directions with the same goal of letting everyone know about the beginning of the Revolutionary War. I say apparently because I had no idea who William Dawes was. The point the authors were making was how much more effective Paul Revere was in his networking ability.

Our society and culture have a great willingness to socially network through Facebook, LinkedIn, texting, and many other means. We have exponential links to good friends and colleagues, and are even willing to connect with many people we barely know—and in many cases people we don't know at all. However, social networking has evolved into its own culture and comfort level for people of all ages. When it comes to networking within your own company, I have found an uncomfortable hesitation among the employee base. We are willing to socially network with virtually millions, but we do not go beyond our own boss or our boss's boss when it could help our career immensely.

When discussing and presenting networking, I often ask how many are in mentor relationships. I usually get a decent response. When I ask the question, "How many of you have met with your mentor within the last month?" most hands go down. I think we feel the comfort of saying we have mentors, but many of these relationships quickly become inactive or dormant. We should maximize all mentor relationships as a networking springboard. Specifically, we should not only be gleaning advice and learning during these sessions, but we should always be asking questions, such as, "Who do you think I can meet with to learn about (fill in any subject here)?" and, "Do you think (fill in leader's name) knows who I am?" If you have a mentor, make it an active relationship and use it to build your network. Why can't we use the same tenacity for professional networking that we might with social networking?

I am not naïve enough to think that company employees do not sit around the water coolers and conference tables talking about people. Much of this conversation is comparing one person to another. Whether the judgments are performance based, potential based, or skills based, these conversations are happening daily all around us. This comment is not to make you paranoid about interacting with others or about being yourself. The comment is to make you realize that each day presents an opportunity for you to promote yourself in the eyes of the people making decisions. It does not mean doing cartwheels up and down the aisles to get someone's attention, but it should cause you to realize that you have a professional obligation to represent the company well, and also present yourself in a way in which you can be recognized and grow. First impressions are lasting. Lasting impressions may be all someone has when your name comes up in a conversation. The key message is to take a proactive approach to building your network and making others aware of what you have to offer.

During one of my mid-year conversations, my manager told me about a conversation that had taken place around a conference table when names were being discussed for future positions. She asked me, "How many of the fifteen leaders around the table did you know?" I thought I did well when I said I knew about twelve of them. She said, "That leaves three leaders you don't know." She then asked, "Of the twelve people you do know, do you truly know them, do you know of them, or do you just know their names?" I said I truly knew maybe half of them. Therefore, my revised number was six out of fifteen people who could adequately make decisions about my future. She said I had work to do.

We continued the conversation. She reversed the questions and asked, "How many around the table know you well enough to speak intelligently about you and what you've accomplished?" The number was embarrassingly low. She emphasized a point I already knew: I had work to do. I instantly built time into my calendar to meet with a senior leader once a month. Every time I have done this, I ask who else I should talk to, and every time I seem to get at least three more names. My list is long, but the effort is worth it and has been extremely beneficial in my growth. I received more calls from senior leaders in the first year of doing this than I had in the previous nineteen years.

My boss shared this story because she was almost burned herself. Her mentor was in on one of those conversations about future moves and my boss's name came up. When her name was mentioned, her immediate manager said nothing. An extremely bright and talented individual was about to have her moment in the sun dismissed either because the manager did not like her, was in a bad mood, was intimidated by her own peers, did not hear the question, or simply just because. We can continue with the excuses all day long, but the point is that none of us can leave all of our eggs in our manager's basket, even if we have the highest regard for that manager. The mentor stepped in and sang her praises. Do you know what your manager would say about you if he or she had a chance? Are you sure? If you do not know that answer, or you are not sure, get to know the answer. There should be no surprises (good or bad). Communicate with your manager…often. What if your manager called out sick that day? Make sure he or she is talking with others about you, too. It is all right to ask this question, if you have built a strong relationship.

You need to set the tone for yourself on these types of settings to significantly increase your control of your own career. Most people are not doing enough to network because they are unsure of the value or definition. Networking is not "kissing up," as some people like to put it. Networking is not even intentional job searching. Networking allows you to understand how to better maneuver through the complexity of the business and the culture by improving partnerships, building bridges, finding integration points, and sharing best practices. Additionally, networking is making you stronger in the eyes of the decision makers and leaders. Unfortunately, all of this takes time and energy. I have found that people begin this trek only after they see a potential job opening arise. By this time, it is often too late.

When I started my first job in which I had no one reporting to me, I enjoyed the freedom of being on my own—until I realized that I had limited power to influence unless I networked and built partnerships. My job was the task force to assess employee attrition. I had no choice but to see the value of networking to get teammate support and assistance to achieve my own goals to keep people from voluntarily leaving the company. I had to hit the circuit and speak to as many managers and frontline people as possible to ensure that I understood their opinions and feelings. Networking was beginning to be fun. There were points of views I would have never come up with on my own. I needed networking, and together with the management team, business partners, and frontline associates in other areas of the company, we were making a collective dent in reducing the number of people voluntarily leaving our company.

So, after you come to the realization that networking is beneficial, the natural question is, "How do you start a conversation with someone you don't know? They're going to think I am crazy. How do I start?" The answer is simple. Be honest and straightforward. Explain what goal you want to accomplish in the meeting. The person you want to network with should understand if your goal is to learn a different part of the business, to meet someone new, to job shadow, or to job search. The reasons may vary, and all are good for your growth. The constant, however, is always coming back to building an exponentially expanding network—make sure this is clearly stated to the person with whom you are meeting.

Networking, if done right, can and should work for you after the meeting has ended.

Two things made the difference for me when I first started networking. The first two people I spoke with told me to contact them in a few months to give them progress reports. I didn't believe them or think it was a real request. When that incredible but nagging boss of mine asked if I had followed up with them yet, I said that I had not. I called them both later that week, and found out they had truly meant it. When I did it, one of them said, "You made my day," while the other said that he was excited about my progress and had already heard about some of my successes. The second thing that made a difference for me was when I thanked one of the people I networked with for his time and told him how much I had learned. He stopped me and said "thank you" to me for investing time with him. He told me that he got just as excited meeting someone new and adding them to his own contact list. In addition, he told me how thrilled he was to share his business story with others. One of my first network contacts said to this person, "You should talk to Tom at some point. I think he may have something to offer to you." He said, "I already did, and I hired him." I was not shopping for a job.

I now understand that the nature of one person talking to another is really one person talking to many others. It is funny how things work when you are proactive and assertive, and even push yourself outside your comfort level just a little bit. Dots quickly get connected and people in your network connect with people outside your network to become a part of it.

Be Yourself—the Paradox

Dress to impress. You are told you are constantly onstage and people are constantly paying attention to you. Your manager is watching your every move. Now, just try to be yourself. We panic and get uptight when our boss's boss asks for something. Thoughts go through our mind, such as, "Will this be good enough for them?" "I need to impress them," and "What do I need to do to get noticed?" When we have senior leaders visit our building, everyone seems to panic. Messages go out to clean up the work areas, and all of a sudden our business-casual dress code goes away and the ties come back out. If the suits and ties aren't on, there are at least blue blazers everywhere.

I used to wonder if I didn't get that last promotion because my shirt was wrinkled that one time. I now can't remember what I wore yesterday, let alone keep track of everyone else. This isn't about how you dress, it is about how you present yourself…everyday. You shouldn't put on an act just because there are special guests. In fact, what message does that send to people who work for you and work with you if you suddenly change? There are higher ranked people out there, so what? The key is to find your personality and be consistent with it. If you like to create a fun-looking environment with decorations all around, why can't your upper management see it? If you made the decision to put it up, why can't it stay up? If you maintain a clean and safe environment all of the time, there shouldn't be a panic the night before someone comes. I learned to rarely fret over my environment because I maintain it on a regular basis and attempt to teach everyone the importance of presenting themselves respectfully everyday, anyway.

I had to learn to stop trying to impress everyone, all the time. I wanted to take care of my manager, take care of my peers, and take care of the people who worked for me. I wanted to be everywhere, all the time, and give everyone what *they* wanted when *they* wanted it. I became disappointed in myself if my boss requested changes or offered suggestions. I took it personally because they were not impressed with my work. I found I tensed up during presentations, used words that were not natural to me, and tended to be over the top in making the effort to ensure that I was noticed.

When we were in the midst of my former company being bought out, I had a choice to work harder and impress more people, or just do my job to the best of my ability. I was concerned about the unknown, but had confidence in my own ability. I found that the stress of this transition brought out personalities I had never seen before. I saw selfishness in some people who wanted all of the glory, I saw people give up, and I saw people who I thought had loyalty to the company turn their heads. It was an interesting time for everyone. However, the ones who impressed me the most were the ones who never changed along the way. I learned a valuable lesson about the importance of being myself. What did I have to worry about? I was comfortable in my own skin and my confidence had been growing. I was always commended for my hard work, so what needed to change? I had feedback given to me on how to improve, and the only challenge I now had was how to implement the feedback and still be myself. I began to understand how I could do that.

I can't tell you how much more satisfied and content I was with my job and the company when I let down my guard enough to be Tom Dowd. I was not Tom Dowd the Banker, or Tom Dowd the Manager, or Tom Dowd (place label here). I was starting to be more engaging and had more personal conversations to get to know people. It wasn't wasting time like I had always thought in the past. I could carry a conversation and I could also balance it with my business needs. I was relating to people, because they were starting to relate to me.

I could attend my child's play, concert, or game on my own terms because I wanted to be there, because I was being myself, knowing that the job would get done. I was building a stronger bond with the people I worked for and worked with, because they knew exactly what they were getting with me. I had the confidence to know what needed to be done at work and when it had to be done. If there was a conflict, I used my strong relationships to talk to my manager about it. I would instill in them enough confidence to know the job would get done, whether it was by delegating or working different hours. That's not trying to impress, that's just getting your job done the right way.

I have never whipped my cell phone out to look busy in the hall, and have never intentionally sent emails at all hours of the night to impress someone. I have also never been accused of not getting my job done on time and I am always cited as doing it with the utmost quality. There is a balance to what I do now. I ensure that I am conscious of my work quality from the beginning and I don't have to panic at the last minute. Work hard. Work smart. Success will take care of itself if you work in the right company and for the right people. If you work in a place where you are constantly on guard, ask yourself, "Is this the right culture for me? Can I be myself?"

Treat Each Day Like an Interview— Another Paradox

In one breath I tell you that you should be yourself; work hard, and things will take care of themselves. In the second breath, I will tell you that every day is an interview. Isn't that contradictory? A good friend of mine, who has years of Human Resource experience, once told me that a job interview is like a first date. You're about to see someone's supposed best and everything he or she has to give. I had an interview recently where the person was a couple minutes late for our discussion. He had no specific reason, and he didn't know a lot about the job. He even mentioned that he was hoping I could tell him about it. He didn't ask for clarity about the role or more details about the job, he wanted me to tell him about the job he applied for. Although some of his answers were decent, and I saw some growth potential, I walked away from what I will describe as an average interview. As much as I wanted to take a chance on him, I also wanted him to put a little more individual effort into what could have been a career-changing moment. If this was his best for our "first date," I should have concerns about what he can do for my team in the future.

The person interviewing, like on a first date, typically will be dressed well (or should be), prepared (or should be), and ready to give you his or her 'A' game. As the person making a hiring decision during an average interview, we sometimes want to justify the candidate's efforts, and hire him anyway. We either have a hiring goal we need to achieve, see something between the lines, or just want to give someone a break. All are legitimate reasons to make a thoughtful decision. As you are making this thoughtful decision, the question needs to be asked of yourself, "You just saw his or her best. Does it go downhill from here?" I have found too many examples of instances when the decision that average was good enough went badly. The person was not a good fit for the company or job. He or she should have given you his or her 'A' game, but we accepted their 'B' or 'C' game, thus setting the expectations and bar lower right off the bat. It may well go downhill from there.

Once you are in the company, the interview process doesn't stop. Your 'A' game shouldn't go away just because you entered the building as an official employee. I know that brand new cars instantly lose their value as soon as you drive them off the lot, but you are not a new car. Your value should grow as you enter the building—every day. Every day you should strive to raise your game. There will be bad days, but you should make an effort to minimize those bad days and strive to add value to the company each day. This includes interactions with people you work with, work for, and the people who work for you. Don't let your guard down and coast for a day. It only starts you down a path of building bad habits.

For example, have you ever been caught off guard when someone started to use profanity because "it's just the two of you." Have you ever been involved in rumor-mill chatter, or bad mouthing a colleague? How about a casual conversation in the hall that turns into a confidential dialogue? You need to realize that you are constantly being watched, listened to, and judged by people at all levels and your reputation is constantly being evaluated.

If someone witnesses your 'B' or 'C' game, it may leave a lasting impression for a while. Every interaction can be viewed as an interview. It doesn't mean you can't have casual or confidential interactions with others; it means be conscious of your actions and words. Every interaction can be a lasting one; make it a good one. Seek to maintain the reputation you want—the reputation that you are making a top-notch effort every day. I am also not encouraging you to be uppity, snobbish, or to act better than anyone else out there. I am, however, saying that we should all set an example for others to emulate. Be a role model. Being your natural self should include all of this.

So, is the message to be constantly on guard and never have fun? No. Regardless of whether you are a company leader, an emerging leader, or someone who just wants to be respected in the workplace, you should competently be aware of your surroundings and actions. You should make the effort to be in control of your actions and understand the impression you are leaving on others. This includes being fun. If you create a professional and fun environment where employees work hard and are rewarded for their efforts, people will take notice and respond. They will make their own effort to be professional, want to have fun, and work hard because they see you doing it. If their leaders are doing it, then it must be all right for them.

Be yourself and bring your 'A' game each day; be aware that you are a potential role model and you can take the lead to set the tone. You may even get noticed by other decision makers who think you would be a great fit in their shop because they are impressed with you, ironically, for what you may consider an everyday event. Treat each day like an interview—it will pay off.

Effective Tools from *Powerful Professional Transformation: Unleashing Leadership Program*

 **Determine What Interviewers Want...
Dealing with Behavior-based Questions**

The art of interviewing has changed over time for both the people asking the questions and those answering them. Many companies have moved to a behavior-based line of questioning to help identify not only the skills the potential employee has used in the past, but what behaviors and tendencies they have that will translate into future job effectiveness. Think about the phrase, "A leopard never changes his spots." Your likelihood to do something in the future can come out in an interview with the right types of questions. Many of these questions are thought-provoking and intentionally want to see how you might think and react in moments of pressure.

The following section will help to prepare you for all types of interviews. When you successfully understand what interviewers are looking for, you can stop guessing and start confidently presenting your story. Too many people interviewing try to answer questions the way they *think* the interviewer wants to hear it. When you take a step back and allow yourself to be you, while meeting the interviewer's wants and needs, you will have a significant advantage.

What Interviewers are looking for:
- Confidence—not the perfect answer
- You to know yourself better than anyone else. Can you confidently answer, "What is your greatest accomplishment?"
- Ability to think quickly on your feet
- Ability to deal with pressure

- Ability to articulate how you can add value to the organization
- Ability to communicate effectively- clear and concise
- Independent thinking
- Examples where you've been a problem solver, not problem dumper
- You to want the job versus wanting to leave your current job
- A positive attitude
- Ability to translate and align your past history successfully to give confidence you can contribute and succeed going forward
- Creative and fresh ideas that differentiate you
- Positive patterns/trends and clear outcomes exhibited in situational and behavioral based answers
- Preparation- you know what you are interviewing for and you have done your homework
- A two-way dialog—not a Q&A
- To get to know the REAL you
- Your story to come alive—*you* to tell your story, not some résumé or thick binder

Pitfalls in an interview…
- Lack of confidence
- Inability to talk about oneself humbly, but confidently
- Shock and surprise with tough questions
- Short answers that lack details or examples
- Long answers that do not answer the question or contain irrelevant details
- Negativity about current role/previous jobs
- Regurgitate past job responsibilities and not key accomplishments and competencies that will show how you will impact the business
- Guessing, making answers up, and trying to answer the way you *think* the interview wants the answer
- Elaborate and forced questions you plucked out from the morning news

- Candidate asking questions at the end of the interview out of obligation versus genuine interest

Preparing for situational-based and behavioral-based interviews:

It's important to have solid examples and situations ready to go. You may not be able to memorize answers, but you can put yourself through an exercise to practice and prepare:

- Could you answer what type of tree you would be? Don't memorize, just know yourself well enough to answer with confidence and elaboration.
- Don't show surprise or be caught off guard by any questions. Confidence is 90 percent of the battle. Your reaction may be just what the interviewer is testing.
- You always want to get to the next place, not leave the current place.
- Watch for negative comments about current or past roles, past bosses, etc.
- Interviewers are skeptical, at times. Do leopards ever change their spots? If you bad mouth past situations, will you be bringing your negativity to them?
- Situations, behaviors, and outcomes show patterns, trends, and history, while exhibiting your communication and leadership skills.

Work Experience / Preparation

- Have you done your homework? What are the company's core values? What does the particular line of business you're interviewing for do?
- What previous job experience are you most proud of and why? How does this tie into the job you are seeking?
- Can you parallel/parlay your past experiences into the new potential role?
- What differentiates you from others? Well thought out differentiating factors can take you from the masses to someone special the company can't do without.

- Can you bring in personal traits that show you have effectively balanced work/life and that you have a strong body and mind?
- In your most recent position, how many times did you achieve your goals?
- Do you know yourself better than your manager- strengths and weaknesses? You better!
- What previous job experience do you feel qualifies you for this position? Why?

Should you ask questions of the interviewer?
- Absolutely! Make the whole situation a conversation—a two-way dialog. If you need clarification/confirmation, ask.
- Have some questions prepared prior to the interview, but be sensitive to timing, situation, and the impact it may have on the flow of the interview.
- Do not ask questions just to be heard. If you have maintained a two-way discussion, most questions may have been answered anyway, so don't feel compelled to ask a prepared list at the end.

Job Stability/Schedule
- Do you have a solid history of coming to work on time every day?
- Do you have gaps in your résumé? Can they be explained (e.g., maternity/paternity leave, unemployed?)
- Describe a time when….
    - you had to be flexible and change with the company
    - you had to deal with a frustrating situation
    - you had to go beyond your normal job responsibilities

Working Well with Others / Customer Situations
- Tell me about a time when…
    - you had to deal with an upset customer
    - you had to deal with difficult peers

- you proactively stepped up as a leader
- you had to deal with a team that had varying perspectives
- you couldn't help a teammate the way that you wanted
- you set a positive example of teamwork
- there was poor morale and you had to drive enthusiasm
- when you tried but failed to be your best
- How competitive are you? Has it ever negatively impacted your job?
- What do you consider to be one of your greatest accomplishments? DO YOU REALIZE THIS QUESTION STUMPS MANY PEOPLE?
- Describe an example of when you were asked to go against your ethical beliefs?

Career Goals / Goal Achievement
- How do you set your goals and what actions do you take to achieve them?
- Tell me about a time when you turned an impossible goal into an achievement.
- Why are you interested in this job? (Are you trying to get out of what you are doing now or into something to broaden your business acumen?)

Are you truly customer focused?
- Tell me a time where you had to compromise your goals to achieve a customer's goal.
- Tell me about a time when you had to go above and beyond what was expected.
- Tell me about a time when you were able to be flexible with products and services to achieve a customer need.
- Give an example of when you couldn't solve a customer's issue and had to escalate it to your manager? (answer shows judgment,

accountability and ownership. You don't want to dump on your manager, but show good sense when you need to move it up)
- Tell me about a time when you had to deal with an upset customer.
- Tell me about a time when you were able to influence a customer to choose something different than their original choice. (Can you persuade and influence, while still getting the customer what they wanted/needed?)

99 References

Blanck, Jennifer L., "When Clubs Mean Business," *Toastmasters Magazine*, August 2013, (page number).

Brubaker, John, *The Coach Approach: Success Strategies From The Locker Room To The Board Room*. The Sport of Business, 2012.

Carlson, Richard, *Don't Sweat the Small Stuff...and it's all small stuff*. New York: Hyperion, 1997.

Ferrazzi, Keith and Tahl Raz, *Never Eat Alone*, Crown Business, 2005.

Fogarty, John. "Proud Mary." In *Bayou Country*. Fantasy Records, 1969.

Grant, Adam, *Give and Take*, Viking Adult, 2013.

Serdula, Donna, *LinkedIn Makeover: Professional Secrets to a POWERFUL LinkedIn Profile*, Bycko Press, 2011.

"SWOT Analysis," Wikipedia: The Free Encyclopedia. Wikimedia Foundation, Inc., accessed September 10, 2013. http://en.wikipedia.org/wiki/SWOT_analysis

Thomas, Sherri, *The Bounce Back: Personal Stories of Bouncing Back Faster and Higher from a Layoff, Re-org or Career Setback*, Booklocker.com, Inc., 2012.

Uzzi, Brian and Shannon Dunlap. How to Build Your Network. Harvard Business Review, December 2005. www.hbr.org.

Transform into Who You Really Want to Be Professionally

If you're interested in the **Powerful Professional Transformation: Unleashing Leadership** program, contact Thomas Dowd Professional Development & Coaching, LLC, at:

Phone: (207) 596-3217
Email: tomdowd@roadrunner.com
Online: www.TransformationTom.com

Sign up for Transformation Tom's newsletter and material at www.TransformationTom.com

The program is effective as a series, a seminar or as individual presentations. Additionally, Tom offers one-on-one coaching sessions.

Programs can be tailored to meet the needs of any organization or individual.

Why this program?
The global economic conditions have created a steep competitive landscape for employers, employees, unemployed, and future employees alike. Employers may need to make cuts and can only keep their best. Employees are competing against each other in order to shine in the eyes of key decision makers. The unemployed and future employees need solid résumés and interviews in order to stand out amongst thousands of others.
This program will prove that those willing to invest in their employees, and those individuals willing to invest in themselves, will differentiate from the masses and impressively influence any organization. The program, **Powerful Professional Transformation: Unleashing Leadership**, is a journey worth taking. Success and satisfaction levels are dependent upon it. Transform yourself into who you really want to be professionally.

Who can benefit?

Corporate employers. Invest in transforming the employee and employer relationship into an engaged and inspired partnership designed to drive the business together.

Stagnant or disengaged employees. Target your focus to re-energize individuals to become aware of their own accountabilities and take action. The evolution will inspire increased success and satisfaction levels, while expediting the climb up the corporate ladder.

Prospective corporate employees. This includes new/future graduates and individuals looking for a competitive edge. Emphasis is placed upon effectively and quickly adapting in the professional world.

In simple terms, anyone connected to a business will find the interactive program valuable, if not needed!

To purchase large quantities of any of Thomas B. Dowd III's books for groups or organizations at a discount, please contact Thomas Dowd Professional Development & Coaching, LLC, using the contact information at the beginning of this section.

Also by Thomas B. Dowd III

The Transformation of a Doubting Thomas: Growing from a Cynic to a Professional in the Corporate World
ISBN: 978-1-938883-06-4

2012 Honorable Mention New England Book Festival in the "Business" category.

During his inconsistent first twenty years in a business environment, author Thomas Dowd learned lessons, both positive and negative, which transformed into shared professional success. Those experiences empower readers to differentiate themselves and work smarter—not harder—to thrive in a chaotic corporate culture that, due to current economic conditions, encourages the employed and unemployed alike to simply try to survive.

Available for purchase at www.transformationtom.com
and online booksellers everywhere.
Available in print and eBook formats.

Also by Thomas B. Dowd III

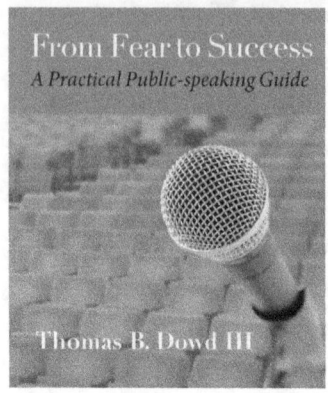

From Fear to Success: A Practical Public-speaking Guide
ISBN: 978-1-938883-04-0

2013 Axiom Business Book Awards Gold Medal in the "Business Reference" category

2013 Honorable Mention Paris Book Festival and New York Book Festivals in the "How-to" and "Business" categories, respectively.

Dizzy head. Pounding heart. Shaking limbs. Sweating body. Shallow breathing. Queasy stomach. These symptoms hold people back from what they really want: SUCCESS. An easy-to-read guide to overcome anxiety and relate to any audience, *From Fear to Success* will resonate with public speakers at all levels on their journey to communication confidence.

Available for purchase at www.transformationtom.com
and online booksellers everywhere.
Available in print, eBook, and audiobook formats.

About the Author

Tom Dowd is a previously unemployed professional like the millions of people over the years who have had to deal with the down-turned economy as it struggled to recover. He used his expertise in the professional development field to land his own job after a tough loss due to budget cuts.

Tom has more than twenty-three years of experience in management and leadership roles in the financial industry, and runs his own business, Thomas Dowd Professional Development & Coaching, LLC. As a speaker, author, trainer and coach, he helps people find ways to creatively differentiate themselves in the workplace and to find their individual paths toward success. The company tagline is: "Transform into who you really want to be professionally."

Starting in 2008 as one of the founding members, Tom was the vice president of education for Dirigo Toastmasters Club in Belfast. He is now a member of the Kennebec Valley Toastmasters Club and Bangor Toastmasters Club. Toastmasters International is a supportive learning environment of more than 270,000 members worldwide designed to improve communication and leadership skills. Tom holds advanced communication and advanced leadership certifications with Toastmasters International, including High Performance Leadership certification. In November 2011, Tom was selected as the District 45 Toastmaster of Year, which represents more than one hundred clubs in the states of Maine, Vermont, and New Hampshire, and the three eastern Canadian provinces of Prince Edward Island, New Brunswick, and Nova Scotia. Tom has also seen consistent success when competing at the division (state level equivalent) and district levels in Toastmasters speech contests, which include humorous, inspirational, impromptu, and evaluation events. He is the two-time Table Topics (impromptu) District 45 Champion (2012 and 2013).

Tom developed a series of management presentations into a speaking program called "Powerful Professional Transformation: Unleashing Leadership." The speaking engagements turned into his first two books. Published in September 2012, both books have since garnered recognition in the business field. *The Transformation of a Doubting Thomas: Growing from a Cynic to a Professional in the Corporate World*, a book detailing Tom's own professional growth based on lessons learned in his career, received honorable mention in the business category at the 2012 New England Book Festival, while *From Fear to Success: A Practical Public-speaking Guide* received the Gold Medal in the Business Reference category at the 2013 Axiom Book Awards, Honorable Mention at the 2013 New York Book Festival, and Honorable Mention at the 2013 Paris Book Festival.

Tom graduated from the University of Delaware in 1990 with a Communication degree, concentrating on interpersonal and organizational communication.

Tom lives in Camden, Maine with his wife and three daughters.

www.ingramcontent.com/pod-product-compliance
Lightning Source LLC
Chambersburg PA
CBHW051652170526
45167CB00001B/429